I0605951

MORE PRAISE FOR *MASTERS OF UNCERTAINTY*

"The Navy SEALs aren't great because they have better tactics or more courage. They're great because they have made a business of outflanking the unpredictable. No one knows these methods better than Rich Diviney. And in this powerfully refined book, they're all here."

—BEN MILLIGAN, former Navy SEAL and bestselling author of *By Water Beneath the Walls. The Rise of the Navy SEALs*

"Rich Diviney isn't just another Navy SEAL with a memoir; he's the expert who has cracked the code for thriving under pressure. *Masters of Uncertainty* brings his two decades of experience to life with actionable strategies. Whether you're navigating a boardroom or a battlefield, Rich shows you how to turn chaos into your greatest asset."

—ED MYLETT, bestselling author, entrepreneur, and host of the critically acclaimed and top-rated podcast *The Ed Mylett Show*

"Rich Diviney's *Masters of Uncertainty* is not just for the military; his strategies apply to everyday, real-world life, empowering people to lead their team or help themselves be resilient and adaptable through life's unpredictable challenges."

—GABBY REECE, former professional volleyball player, bestselling author, and host of *The Gabby Reece Show* podcast

"*Masters of Uncertainty* is a how-to manual for thriving during chaos. Rich Diviney has written another very important addition to the human performance canon. A great read!"

—**STEVEN KOTLER,** *New York Times* bestselling author of *Art of Impossible* and executive director of the Flow Research Collective

"If anyone knows how to navigate the unpredictable, it's Rich Diviney. In *Masters of Uncertainty,* he breaks down what it really takes to perform under stress, and his insights are as valuable in everyday life as they are in combat. This book is essential reading for anyone who wants to stay calm and effective, no matter what comes their way."

—**DANIEL COYLE,** *New York Times* bestselling author of *The Culture Code* and *The Talent Code*

"In a lifetime of practicing, teaching, and studying the art of leadership, I don't know of a thought leader in the space who brings a more nuanced view on the topic than Rich Diviney, a leader who has always challenged those around him to think differently. *Masters of Uncertainty* is another must-read from Diviney for any leader looking for thought-provoking, accessible, and implementable steps to enhancing performance."

—**CHRIS FUSSELL,** former Navy SEAL, bestselling author, and vice chairman of the McChrystal Group

www.amplifypublishinggroup.com

Masters of Uncertainty: The Navy SEAL Way to Turn Stress into Success for You and Your Team

For more information, please contact:
Amplify Publishing, an imprint of Amplify Publishing Group
620 Herndon Parkway, Suite 220
Herndon, VA 20170
info@amplifypublishing.com

Library of Congress Control Number: 2024919429

CPSIA Code: PRV1124A

ISBN-13: 979-8-89138-399-9

Printed in the United States

For all those striving
to unleash their full potential

MASTERS OF

UNCERTAINTY

The Navy SEAL Way to
Turn Stress into Success
for You and Your Team

RICH DIVINEY

CONTENTS

“Uncertainty is the very condition to impel man to unfold his powers.”

—ERICH FROMM

FOREWORD

There are those among us who harbor special knowledge—wisdom, skills, and insights that, if understood, can vastly transform our lives for the better. These people are not Jedi, superheroes, or mystics. I'm talking about real people who are grounded in real, everyday life and yet view the world and the experience of being human differently enough to somehow navigate with far more grace and effectiveness than 99.9 percent of other people—over and over, and regardless of the conditions they happen to find themselves in.

These people don't just "grind"—in fact, they never seem to grind at all, and they are not about learning how to "just not give a damn." They sleep, but they also juggle a ton. They are serious yet maintain a sense of levity, energy, and optimism that seems to afford them more energy and optimism. They are confident, kind, and rarely complain. Life just seems more tractable for them. They make the difficult seem easy. They are deeply confident.

What makes these people even more rare is that they also harbor a deep desire to share their knowledge with others. They genuinely love people and know they have something valuable to teach. In an ocean of advice-giving gurus, business-tactic strategists, and ex-pro-athlete inspirational storytellers, this group stands out. They are peerless. So who are these incredible people, and how can you meet and learn from them?

Enter Rich Diviney, former Tier-1 Navy SEAL (translated: elite of the elite warfighter), family man, business founder, and leader—and known among his friends and family as a deeply kind and driven "giver." I met Rich in 2017 and, like most civilians who meet SEALs for the first time, was hoping for an inside scoop, not about a former mission (they won't tell you anyway) but about how one can focus and reset their mind toward the mission-critical task of everyday living. I wanted to understand how Rich viewed and navigated the world that the rest of us live in. And whenever we spoke together at the same gatherings, it was clear that most everyone in the audience was wondering the same thing.

What ensued between us was a series of long discussions over meals and coffee where Rich came to formalize, literally chart out, how to master the most daunting enemy of all—yet the one we all face: uncertainty. This book is a practical guide for how to wake up and be the most effective version of yourself, how to bring that to all your life's challenges, and (most importantly) how to perpetually bounce upward and forward when pushed back or under pressure . . . and in so doing, exceed your previous self and performance—over and over and over. And therein lies the magic and uniqueness of *Masters of Uncertainty*.

In the pages that follow, you'll learn a way of thinking about life that is simple and structured enough to make perfect sense yet dynamic and effective enough to be applied to any situation. Truly, *any* situation. Diviney explains and walks you through it, teaching you to frame your life through the lens of what works in the most high-risk, high-consequence situations but applied to meet your unique life challenges and goals. As I started by saying, people like Rich Diviney are rare: because of what they know, for what they have proved capable of doing, and for their ability to teach it to others . . . and now to you.

This book will powerfully shift how you view and approach life—its challenges and its less challenging moments too—for the better. Of that, I am certain.

Andrew D. Huberman, PhD
September 2024

INTRODUCTION

UNCERTAINTY IS THE ONLY CERTAINTY

On May 2, 2011, a team of US Navy SEALs set forth on one of the most audacious missions in modern combat history. Their objective: To capture or kill Osama bin Laden, the architect of the September 11 atrocities. After a decade-long manhunt, an intricate tapestry of intelligence-gathering by various agencies had pinpointed bin Laden's lair.

Briefed weeks in advance, the team delved into rigorous preparations. They constructed an exact replica of the compound for meticulous drills. They memorized the mission's choreography to the minutest detail.

Yet immediately upon arrival, the plan had to change. A helicopter crashed; entry proved more challenging and time-consuming than planned, and the timeline got skewed.

The critical advantages of stealth and haste evaporated into the night. After exhaustive drills and strategy sessions, the team was thrust into the chasm of uncertainty.

The finale, however, is etched in history.

Osama bin Laden was neutralized, with the SEALs returning unscathed, a testament to their adaptability and prowess. The mission stands as a paragon of exceptional execution, universally acclaimed for its precision and effectiveness.

But while the SEALs' ability to train and strategize is unparalleled, what sets them apart isn't just martial skill or strategic acumen. It's their composure amid the unpredictable, their deft navigation through complexity and chaos. They are not just sharpshooters, parachutists, or divers; they are virtuosos of volatility, capable of performance not only when the seas are calm but also—and perhaps more importantly—when plunged into the tumultuous depths of disorder and upheaval.

They are Masters of Uncertainty.

The operation to neutralize bin Laden was not a deviation but a testament to their standard: SEALs are known to deliver, regardless of the hurdles. Their very ethos is to surmount the insurmountable, to turn the tide in the face of the unforeseen. This mission was a demonstration of supreme achievement—realizing their objective amid a maelstrom of the unforeseen.

Impressive, isn't it?

Yet not beyond reach. Navy SEALs, after all, are human too.

SUCCESS ISN'T SUPERHUMAN

If there is one certainty in life, it's that uncertainty shows up for all of us.

Consider these scenarios:

- Your pulse accelerates, the aftermath of a critical call with a client resonating in your chest. They're facing a system meltdown, their words a veiled ultimatum to your contract. The clock hands align at 5:00 p.m., the office deserted and the company's fate seemingly teetering on the edge. In stressful moments like these, what's your strategy for success?

- An unexpected call pierces your routine: a loved one hospitalized, the urgency palpable. Keys in hand, you're already in motion, the car's engine humming in tandem with your thoughts. As you navigate the roads, strategic questions surface—second opinions, hospital choices. You're propelled not just by the engine but also by a torrent of racing thoughts, plotting paths around potential pitfalls. How do you manage the onslaught?

- The pivotal moment unfolds: a spotlight illuminates you standing on stage alone, about to give your long-anticipated presentation. Weeks of preparation, of rehearsals in solitude, converge here. Despite tremors that threaten to betray your composure, you stand before the audience ready to go. Then a curveball: the audio and visual aids have failed, leaving you unaccompanied by notes and slides. Yet the audience's gaze is fixed, awaiting your voice—unfettered by the technical tether. What happens next?

In such moments, how have you navigated the tides? How *would* you navigate the tides? Would the outcome align with your hopes? The best-laid plans often meet with faltering, missteps, and miscalculations. Would you succumb to thoughtless instinct? Many follow a siren call to delay action or to tumble into a rush of panic, inadvertently compounding their challenges. Some relinquish their grip midjourney or forgo embarking at all, daunted by self-doubt or the magnitude of what's at stake.

Unfortunately, falling short under stress is the norm, not the exception, a shared human refrain.

Most people fall short of realizing their potential primarily because our culture promotes a misleading belief: that life is predictable.

It's not your fault if you succumb to this fallacy. Seeking to predict and prepare for the future stems from a fundamental human need for certainty. Our society, brimming with instant-gratification apps and round-the-clock services, ensures our needs are constantly met. Our everyday experiences, from banking transactions to restaurant bookings, are designed for smooth, convenient consistency. This reality has given rise to what I term "the predictability paradigm," a subtle yet pervasive belief that life will unfurl as anticipated.

However, expecting life to adhere to our blueprints sets us up for turmoil when the unforeseen occurs—as it regularly does, in both significant and minor ways. Such instances throw us off-balance, leading to disarray and, at times, panic. They force us to recalibrate, adapt, and often struggle to recover our footing.

THE DECEIT OF PEAK PERFORMANCE

Arguably, the most detrimental aspect of the predictability paradigm is its reinforcement of the notion that peak performance represents the ultimate standard of success. Peak performance, however, is performance at the highest possible level, so it is just that—a peak, an apex from which there is nowhere to go but down. Peak performance is often conditional. It typically requires a predictable and familiar environment. It requires training, discipline, and preparation. A professional football player will design his entire week's schedule so that he can peak for three hours on Sunday.

In reality, repetitive peak performance is unrealistic because uncertainty is life's foundational state. The unpredictable is ever-present, waiting just around the bend. It can arise at any moment, in any magnitude, from any quarter. Striving for peak performance or even expecting yourself to always perform to the perfect standards of "peak" as a constant goal sets the stage for setbacks when faced with the unpredictable.

True success in life and business hinges instead on optimal performance, which means delivering your "best" in the moment, whatever your best looks like in that moment. At times, your best aligns with peak performance, where everything is clicking and things seamlessly fall into place. However, sometimes your best is about persevering, moving forward step-by-step in the midst of challenges, embracing the messy, grueling, and unpolished reality. Genuine success is about maintaining optimal performance in all conditions—not solely when things are smooth but also amid unpredictability and when uncertainty is rife.

If you want to succeed in business and in life, you must embrace the truth:

Uncertainty is everywhere all the time, and success is about being able to optimally perform in it.

DESIGNED FOR UNCERTAINTY

What if I told you that your past stumbles were merely echoes, not edicts, of your potential? Imagine what's possible if you unleash the natural (but perhaps latent) prowess within you, akin to the SEALs achieving their caliber of precision and resolve. Now imagine what's possible when this intrinsic ability is not just developed in you but in every team you're part of. Consider the possibility of transforming life's trials into triumphs. You can consistently steer through frustrations and setbacks, always maximizing the chances of success.

Navy SEALs and other high achievers (anyone who is adept in any circumstance) are fundamentally similar to everyone else. Their edge is simply that they harness innate, yet often overlooked, capabilities that we all possess. As Masters of Uncertainty, they are well-practiced experts of navigating the intrinsic unpredictability of life—and you can be one too. It merely requires a shift in perspective and applying one method that enables you to invigorate a suite of innate talents already within your grasp.

Mastering uncertainty isn't akin to wielding a superpower. Over a decade of coaching elite performers, including Navy SEALs, has shown me that their standout performance doesn't stem from mysterious talents.

I've discovered that human performance pivots on six key factors. Three are inherent abilities we all share. Three are unique elements of who we are. Consciously harnessing these factors is the real game changer. Regardless of how you view your current abilities, you have the potential to expertly navigate the tumultuous seas of life and business. You're capable of elevating your performance, regardless of the scale or unpredictability of what you face.

The good news is that you're already somewhat acquainted with these six factors. They're so intrinsic to our nature that you've almost surely employed them subconsciously. You've likely done this recently, possibly even today. However, like many, you've probably not fully tapped into them, leaving them dormant and underdeveloped.

Fortunately, I have the methodology and you possess the capability to start rewriting this narrative today.

THE MASTERING UNCERTAINTY METHOD

For the last decade-plus, I've worked hard to articulate and fine-tune the Mastering Uncertainty Method to be able to not only implement it more in my life but also share it with the world. It's a journey that started with the Navy SEALs and later expanded to top-tier performers across various domains. This approach is structured around six key steps, each tied to either an inherent ability or an insight that's been overshadowed by our misplaced focus on peak performance.

In part I, I delve into reactivating inherent capabilities through three steps. The initial step, Move Horizons, involves consciously deciding upon and executing the most effective action. This is the cornerstone of consistent goal realization and success. The second step, Keep Going, harnesses your body's intrinsic motivation mechanisms to power you through challenges for as long as necessary. The third step, Stay Cool, encompasses a series of practical techniques designed to maintain an optimal balance of alertness and composure, ensuring mental clarity and optimal performance in any situation.

Part II focuses on gaining and applying three vital insights about your fundamental self—your attributes, your identities, and your objectives. We often like to think that we will always act in accordance with the skills, values, and beliefs we carefully cultivate. However, in the face of uncertainty, these things often recede. It's the unvarnished, elemental you that surges to the fore, influencing three critical aspects of performance: what you instinctively do (chapter 5), how you instinctively do it (chapter 4), and why you instinctively do it (chapter 6). Understanding these elemental aspects of yourself equips you and your team to make effective decisions in real time, steering you efficiently toward your objectives and ensuring you attain them regularly.

In part III, I explain how to apply these six steps within team dynamics, guiding groups on their journeys to master uncertainty and sail beyond previous standards of performance.

In chapter 7, I outline the implementation process for dynamic subordination. Chapter 8 explains how to cultivate the essential trust needed for this model to thrive. Finally, chapter 9 describes how to transition into and sustain a dynamically subordinating team culture, which is pivotal for enduring high performance and success.

Ever since introducing the method, I've observed its transformative impact on hundreds of groups. Teams have fostered deeper trust, enhanced adaptability, and seen notable improvements in retention and satisfaction rates. They've learned to navigate challenges as proficiently as they ride waves of success, ensuring they don't just reach the top but also maintain that position.

It's also a method that I've applied to my life. The principles have become integral to my approach in multiple facets, from significant to mundane. My proficiency has enhanced not only in handling crises but also in supporting my family, processing adverse news, navigating traffic, and chasing personal aspirations like entrepreneurship. Overall, my life's performance has improved, and so has my experience of it. I find myself less frustrated, more confident, more at peace, and consistently prepared to present the best version of myself.

The same can happen for you, both as an individual and in your teams.

Both you and any team you are part of inherently possess the capacity to turn the stress of uncertainty into success. Embrace these six steps. Rediscover and harness your innate abilities and insights. Break free from conventional methods. Surpass previous standards and embark on a journey of increased fluidity, adaptability, performance, and success.

Become a Master of Uncertainty!

PART I

MASTERING YOUR ABILITIES

It's tempting to elevate high performers to almost mythical status, viewing their accomplishments as unattainable.

However, this perspective is flawed. High performers are human, just like everyone else. They face challenges, occasionally doubt their abilities, and sometimes revert to old habits of panic, procrastination, or feelings of overwhelm by circumstances.

The cornerstone of their consistent success is action. This can be physical practice, deep thought, reflection, or real-world experience. These Masters of Uncertainty engage in such actions so persistently and thoroughly that it becomes second nature. And so can you.

In this section, I'll delve into the first three steps of the Mastering Uncertainty Method. These fundamental human abilities empower you to navigate uncertainty and thrive in any situation.

- First, **move horizons:** how to remain grounded in the present while taking strategic steps toward your goals.

- Second, **keep going:** how to continue pushing toward these goals, no matter how daunting or overwhelming the task.

- Third, **stay cool:** how to regulate your body's stress response, optimizing your mental and physical energy for any task at hand.

As you explore these strategies, you might recognize moments when you've already utilized them, perhaps without realizing it. We all have these abilities inherently. The key is to deepen your understanding and then take deliberate action. Embrace your natural talents. Unlock your potential. Elevate your performance amid uncertainty, challenges, and stress. And then strive for even greater levels of excellence.

CHAPTER 1

MOVE HORIZONS

The Natural Process That Keeps You in Control

Uncertainty strikes.

You miss a flight. A trusted team member bows out without warning. A collision snarls the highway, threatening your punctuality for a crucial meeting.

Your physiology kicks in. It's a primal, uncontrollable reaction, outpacing thought. Vision tunnels; heartbeat ticks up; thoughts race.

Welcome to autonomic arousal—a.k.a. the stress response.

How do you react?

FLIP THE SCRIPT: FROM STRESSED TO STIMULATED

Our culture seldom sees stress as an opportunity. It's uncomfortable and therefore unwanted. Itching for relief, we often react instinctively and counterproductively in two ways: panic or procrastination.

Panic happens when the discomfort becomes so intolerable that you're driven to quell it impulsively, forgoing the wisdom of a measured breath. You fail to consult the compass of your knowledge and influence, and you lash out blindly at the situation, hoping to nudge the needle closer to your desired outcome. Yet often this hastiness breeds more of the very chaos you sought to escape. In the irony of such high-stakes moments, you compound the chaos, creating fresh fodder for even more panic.

Procrastination happens when the discomfort of autonomic arousal, or even just your *anticipation* of it, makes the task seem too daunting to confront head-on. You take refuge in diversion and distraction, while deep down secretly harboring hope that the trouble will untangle itself. But this seldom happens. The situation typically gathers momentum and becomes more urgent while, beneath the surface, you remain tethered to the turmoil. Undercurrents of stress and anxiety swell. The irony is not lost: in seeking to sidestep the storm, you inadvertently brew a greater one. You feed the cycle that fueled your initial avoidance.

But it doesn't have to be this way. In fact, it wasn't *meant* to be this way.

In truth, autonomic arousal is a call to arms. It's a mobilizing force. It's your body offering you alertness and energy meant to equip you to tackle perceived threats.

The great news is that you're innately prepared to transform this stress response from a hindrance that hurts your performance into a surge of vitality that propels it forward. You can embrace and channel your body's energy, pairing it with composure and strategic control.

How? By tapping into a primal capability you already possess that I call "moving horizons." Moving horizons is a process where you anchor yourself in the present moment by focusing on what you can ascertain and influence. You use what you already know and control to learn more and to steer events toward your desired result.

The essence of moving horizons is being both swift and proactive. Swift, because when unchecked, autonomic arousal escalates, impairing performance and fueling panic or delay. Proactive, because establishing control from the onset is far more manageable than fighting to regain lost ground.

DURATION, PATHWAY, OUTCOME

When uncertainty, challenge, or stress strike, autonomic arousal starts its climb. But have you ever wondered about its roots? It all starts with the brain, which gauges the levels of uncertainty in a scenario by considering three key factors:

1. **Duration:** The ticking clock—how long this episode will stretch.
2. **Pathway:** The road map—your passage through it.
3. **Outcome:** The finish line—what lies at the end of the road.

Autonomic arousal fires in proportion to how clear the brain is on these three aspects of a situation. Lacking clarity on one element nudges you into mild arousal. Lacking clarity on two escalates you to moderate. Void of all three, you may find yourself on the brink of high arousal, perhaps teetering toward overload.

Consider the relatable ordeal of being ensnared in traffic when running late for an important meeting.

What's known: Pathway and Outcome.
What's unknown: Duration.

Picture yourself gridlocked. There's no detour in sight. Yet the culprit—a stalled car—is being moved to the side of the road. Here, you have a pathway: the clearing road, and you have an outcome: traffic will dissipate—but how long will that take? The duration eludes you. You don't know how long it'll take. Uncertainty is present, albeit at a relatively low level.

Now erase another detail.

What's known: Outcome.
What's unknown: Duration and Pathway.

Immobile, no exits in sight, the road's fate ahead hidden from view—your pathway has vanished. Yet your navigation app assures you of a clear path two miles ahead. The outcome remains intact, so uncertainty sits at a medium pitch.

Now erase one more.

What's known: Nothing.
What's unknown: Duration, Pathway, and Outcome.

Here you are, stranded with no escape, no visibility ahead, and silence from your app. With drivers emerging from their vehicles, it seems possible that you could be stuck interminably, and the level of uncertainty peaks, for all three elements have deserted you.

Moving horizons is a process where you remain anchored in the present while actively shaping your own Duration, Pathway, and Outcome. Life's unpredictability often leaves us without clear timelines, defined steps, or guaranteed outcomes for our challenges. This lack of clarity can lead to a whirlwind of uncertainty and escalating stress. However, embracing the moving horizons philosophy empowers you to forge certainty amid ambiguity. You take the helm, crafting your own DPO—Duration, Pathway, and Outcome.

Here's the strategy.

> Plant your feet firmly in the present. Ask: "What do I know and control right now?" Then carve out a DPO by selecting a goal within reach. Marching toward this self-made DPO not only propels you forward but also rewards you with a burst of dopamine to help keep you going (see chapter 2). It's a cycle: Pose the question, set the DPO, advance. Pose the question, set the DPO, advance.
>
> Step-by-step, you continue to assess, then act, based on the current information. While you're cognizant of your ultimate aim, you're not burdened by it; your focus remains on the present, on what you know and can influence in that moment. Then, incrementally, you expand your domain of control, advancing toward your

goal while staying firmly in the now. No spiraling into doomsday scenarios or needless panic. You focus on what's at hand, empowering you to make meaningful choices amid uncertainty.

Sound familiar? Chances are, you've done it before—caught in a traffic snarl, blindsided by a sudden pivot at work, stood up by friends, or just navigating the ebb and flow of daily life's caprice. You've successfully realized your goal, nonetheless, by breaking it down into singular DPOs to concentrate on sequentially. And it's not just in the face of uncertainty; even when the road seems clear, like powering through a demanding workout, you've probably homed in on completing just one set at a time, instead of being daunted by the entire regimen.

This is the essence of advancing your horizons and forging your own Duration, Pathway, and Outcome—a skill ingrained in our very nature. It's the brain's way of eating the proverbial elephant, one bite at a time, or segmenting surroundings into manageable morsels. The key is to harness this instinct with intent and precision.

Moving horizons is the process of moving one step at a time through uncertainty. It's consciously staying focused on what you know and can control in the present moment, creating a DPO to move to, moving to it, and then repeating the process. You sequentially grow the sphere of what you know and control. This is done until one or more of the following has occurred:

1. There's no uncertainty left.
2. You've moved through the challenge or stress.
3. You've achieved your goal.

I name these increments "horizons" because you approach each one in turn. You deliberate on one choice in each moment. You undertake one deed at a time. You voyage from one horizon to the next until at last you emerge into tranquil seas with the venture concluded and the aim, more often than not, attained.

CONTROL IN THE PRESENT MOMENT

The domain of what you know and control in the present moment is the anchor for those who master uncertainty. Whenever doubt beckons, identify it by asking, "What do I know? What can I control?" Doubt emerges from many places, but the most common are worry, overwhelm, and the urge to panic.

Amplify your performance with three additional ideas:

1. The Difference between Planning and Worrying

You must anticipate possible eventualities and devise contingency plans, always with an eye on how present actions might ripple into the future. Yet this is best done with deliberate and tactical thought. Once you've navigated through your thoughts, don't dwell. Don't obsessively rehash or spiral into asking increasingly unlikely "what-ifs." That's *worry*. When you find yourself ensnared in worry, stop immediately and shift your focus to the tangible and manageable elements of the now. You can help yourself do this with the sensory and breath work practices I offer in chapter 3.

2. Accept Your Limits

There's a lot going on, and it might seem challenging, maybe overwhelming, to get your hands around everything. That's okay—because you *can't*. Mastering uncertainty doesn't mean you control everything and do everything perfectly. It means you perform optimally: you cultivate innate talents like moving horizons to empower you to do your best. Theoretically, even if you could get your hands around everything in one instant, situations evolve. The unpredictable always lurks.

So don't despair over your lack of total control. Embrace and grow that which you *do* control. Anchor yourself in the present and ensure your knowledge is current. Equip yourself to make the most informed decisions for the here and now. The ability to adapt based on current information is key to navigating through uncertainty with strategic grace.

3. Help Your Brain Help You

The frontal lobe is the part of the brain that thinks coolly and executes strategically considered steps even while other parts of you might be inclined to follow panicked instinct. When the frontal lobe is in command, actions are considered, not just reflexive. Knowledge and control are the reins that guide your frontal lobe and are therefore your bulwark, keeping the surges of instinctual response from overwhelming your composure. Return your focus to what you know and control, and you empower your frontal lobe to do its job of thinking and acting as rationally as possible.

Remember: the heart of unease in uncertain times often lies in the void of not knowing. Consider a situation like when rumors of layoffs ripple about the workplace. It's a haze of speculation with no clear source.

You're in the dark about where these whispers originated, who might be at risk, or the reliability of such claims (worry). It's human nature to envision a kaleidoscope of disastrous outcomes (causing overwhelm). Instinct might provoke a hasty response (panic), like firing off heated emails to management, a move that could escalate your predicament.

But what if the rumors are unfounded or you're not even on the proverbial hit list? Center yourself with these questions: "What do I truly know? What can I control?" Bypass impulsive actions and instead seek out intelligence that enables you to move through the situation in a measured and informed manner.

ACTUALIZE YOUR NEUROLOGY WITH BETTER QUESTIONS

To remain grounded in the sphere of what you know and control, cultivate a habit of asking yourself better questions. The brain operates with a question-answer mechanism: it continuously assesses the surroundings with questions and then conjures answers. This typically happens subliminally and instantly, faster than you can notice. You can, however, participate consciously in this process and influence your thoughts and feelings by introducing your own questions.

When you introduce a question into conscious thought, the mind is compelled to come up with answers. The problem is that it's all too common to default to reactive, negative, and sometimes emotion-laden questions such as "Why am I so bad at this?" or "Why can't I succeed?" Your brain will immediately begin to give you answers to these—yet the answers will not lead to enlightenment. Rather, they will spiral you into further negativity and anxiety.

Masters of Uncertainty steer their thoughts with better, more effective questions—questions that center on what they can ascertain and influence. Well aware that knowledge morphs into power, they prime their minds with inquiries like "What do I know? What can I control?" The brain can't help but answer these questions in ways that put *you* at the helm. These are the inquiries that empower and hone your focus on traversing uncertainty, not succumbing to it.

These strategies are what I like to refer to as "actualizing neurology." Masters of Uncertainty aren't inherently different from the rest of us; they're simply tapping into the preexisting capabilities of their brains. They harness the power of the mind by taking the reins, asking the right questions, and anchoring themselves firmly in the now. These individuals pilot their courses through life with a steadfast belief in their own command. They engage their neurology from a stance of empowerment and deliberate action. By leveraging the insights their brains offer, they adeptly shift horizons and realize their full performance potential.

KEY POINTS: CHAPTER 1

1. **Transform Stress:** The stress response is designed by nature to get us up and moving. You can use stress as a source of energy and alertness. Transform it into a positive force that empowers you to avoid the pitfalls of procrastination and panic.

2. **Moving Horizons:** Navigate stress, challenge, and uncertainty by focusing on what is within your immediate knowledge and control. Set your own DPO. Move to the horizon. Set the next DPO. Move to the horizon. Repeat.

3. **Practice:** Apply the moving horizons technique in everyday situations like traffic jams or sudden changes in the workplace. Stay focused on the present and what you can control, avoiding unnecessary worry and panic.

4. **Ask Yourself Better Questions:** Harness the brain's question-answer mechanism by recognizing the importance of asking effective questions that maintain control and focus on empowering results.

CHAPTER 2

KEEP GOING

Your Body's Performance Generator

I ONCE GAVE A TALK at a conference where I encountered George. George was an ultrarunner. I knew from my own history of running during my Navy days that ultrarunning is about as challenging as it can get. Ultrarunners compete in events over fifty miles, meaning their training often includes running marathons just for practice. But more striking than his endurance feats was his personal transformation. George hadn't just reached the world's top tier of endurance running. He had started his journey to it weighing 450 pounds.

Running was more than a sport for George; it was part of a significant weight-loss journey—a journey often beset with self-doubt and overwhelm. *How did he do it? How did he achieve such a remarkable transformation?* George leveraged what was already there lying latent, ready to help. It was him tapping into the body's innate motivation system. He began creating current DPOs and setting horizons to address present uncertainties. That's the foundation of drive.

But there is one more factor he applied to the process to make it work. It wasn't sheer determination, passion, or grit (though they were a part of the mix). George created *meaningful* horizons.

THE "GRIT MYTH"

Many harbor a misconception I refer to as the "grit myth": the belief that sheer willpower and unyielding effort are the keys to overcoming challenges, as if depleting one's energy is a badge of honor. They often assume high achievers have an almost supernatural amount of stamina that exceeds normal bounds.

This is a fallacy. Relying on raw grit alone is a finite game that inevitably leads to exhaustion or even burnout (which often precludes quitting altogether). Those who navigate uncertainty and sustained efforts with finesse do not depend solely on grit or even on determination or passion.

To truly harness motivation, one must *appropriately* engage the body's inherent drive system. This concept, combined with the strategy of moving horizons, resonates on a profound, instinctual level. You've experienced its efficacy in your own life, perhaps unconsciously, in your endeavors and in weathering uncertainty. Gaining a deeper understanding of this system and your interplay with it equips you to establish horizons that are optimally sized, sustaining your momentum through any trial or uncertain times, for however long the journey demands.

SET MEANINGFUL HORIZONS

Moving horizons naturally supports drive because it anchors attention in the immediacy of the now, warding off the paralysis of overwhelm.

I was able to pass through the grueling crucible of SEAL training's Hell Week partly because of how steadfastly I glued my attention to the present moment. I eschewed any temptation to cast my thoughts toward the finish line and instead concentrated exclusively on what lay within my immediate grasp of knowledge and influence. This conserved my mental and emotional reserves even after my physical body had been pushed beyond its limits. Yet there's another trick that elevates perseverance and drive to guarantee success: setting *meaningful* horizons.

A meaningful horizon is judiciously sized. It's a challenge that's within reach yet still calls for a stretch. It's that sweet spot just beyond the borders of your comfort zone. It possesses a Duration, Pathway, and Outcome that are attainable, yet it demands a measure of exertion. It's the kind of goal that sparks a reassuring "Yes, I've got this!" and rewards you with a fulfilling nod of achievement upon completion.

This is precisely the strategy George employed. He began by buying a pair of running shoes. The next day, he put them on. The next day he went as far as the door, and the next day to the mailbox, and then the next to the end of the street. Each day, George pushed his boundaries just a little, setting and achieving incremental yet impactful goals. Two years from the start, he was racing through the finish line of his first marathon.

Each day, George intentionally reflected on the ground he'd covered the day before. He set a fresh horizon that struck the perfect balance of challenge. His daily targets were strategically calibrated—not too simple, but never too daunting. They nudged him incrementally beyond his last accomplishment, instilling confidence that he could indeed stretch just a bit further—and he consistently did. Each horizon George reached, while sometimes small, was also significant, providing a gratifying sense of progress that propelled him forward.

I had this epiphany during my own SEAL Training Hell Week. One of our trials was to endure what is called "surf torture": to lie in the bone-chilling surf zone for hours without any indication of when it would end.

Amid my own gasping for breath, numbness creeping into my limbs, and muscles searing with pain, I realized that imagining the end or convincing myself to stick it out until it was over felt overwhelming. At the same time, aiming to persist for mere seconds felt trivial. But setting my sights on the next two minutes, or enduring the next ten waves, were two ways to set a horizon of just the right size: challenging but attainable. I knew I could withstand two minutes, so I'd withstand two minutes. After that I'd withstand two more, or however many seemed a challenging but attainable amount in that moment. After reaching each horizon, I would set another. I kept up this strategy until the end.

DOPAMINE AND THE MOTIVATION BALANCE

Meaningful goals boost, rather than drain, motivation because of how dopamine functions. Often dubbed the molecule of "pleasure" or "reward," dopamine does create a feeling of reward for pleasurable activities. Yes, it spikes when you indulge in something like a tasty dessert. But there's more to it. Dopamine is actually the driving force that enables you to seek out pleasurable experiences in the first place. It is the motivational push behind the pursuit of rewarding things. It powers the pursuit of *all* goals, from getting a slice of cheesecake to enduring surf torture.

But here's the catch: if a goal seems too daunting, your body can't produce enough dopamine to propel you toward it. You end up feeling unmotivated, exhausting your willpower, and perhaps faltering, quitting, or failing. Picture standing at the base of a mountain with a thousand steps cut into it. That's a hefty number. Could you manage it? If you set your sights on the full one thousand steps, it might seem too intimidating to even start. Or maybe you lose steam after ten or one hundred steps as overwhelm mounts and your dopamine progressively dwindles. Of course, this all depends on your physical condition and whether the goal aligns with your abilities. A seasoned climber, for example, might breeze through those one thousand steps, dopamine pumping smooth and steady.

On the flip side, if your goal is too modest, the feeling of reward when you achieve it will be minimal or even zero. Imagine going up just half a flight of stairs, which is usually about six steps. If this is not an achievement for you but just a rote part of daily life, your dopamine levels will not rise when you complete this objective. There's no noticeable achievement, so there will be no noticeable reward. If you expect a burst of satisfaction from the activity, you will be sorely disappointed, and you'll likely end up feeling unfulfilled and lethargic. You might just end up plopping down to watch TV instead. Of course, what you experience on this flight of stairs also depends on your physical condition and whether the goal aligns with your abilities. If you've just recovered from a surgery or are on a major weight loss journey, six steps could be an accomplishment that gives you a burst of satisfaction when you complete it. Meaningful horizons are always subjective to the individual and current situation.

If you find yourself overwhelmed at the outset or give up midway through a goal that's too ambitious, don't be too hard on yourself. It's not necessarily a lack of willpower. It's more about your dopamine system reaching its limit. That sinking feeling of "I can't do this" is your dwindling dopamine speaking. It's unable to power you to a goal that is seemingly unattainable. When this happens, pause and consider how you might set a feasible yet rewarding horizon for this immediate moment.

MEANINGFUL HORIZONS KEEP YOU GOING

Meaningful horizons are always personal, calibrated to your own abilities. The dopamine system fires according to what feels like accomplishment to *you*. This is a part of why establishing your own DPOs during uncertainty is so effective: you set tasks according to what *you* can do, at *that* point in time.

Select a horizon that's within your reach—one that you can not only achieve but also use as a stepping stone to continue your journey. This is the approach I took in the surf and George with his running. We each chose horizons of significant but manageable size, reaping the satisfaction of accomplishment and harnessing that momentum to establish and pursue the next horizon. The art of navigating any challenge lies in connecting one meaningful horizon to the next.

Craft a challenge that's genuine yet measured—intense enough to light that inner fire but not so daunting that it extinguishes it. The surge of dopamine from conquering each meaningful horizon is the fuel that will launch you toward the next one.

KEEP YOUR EYES *OFF* THE PRIZE

Feeling overwhelmed is a surefire way to deplete dopamine, which is why the old adage "Keep your eyes on the prize" can sometimes backfire.

Whenever you fixate on the end point of a challenge, you unknowingly pile on stress about all the effort you anticipate having to exert to get there. Have you ever found yourself in the midst of a tough workout, glanced at how much time is left, and suddenly felt the need to muster extra willpower to continue? Looking ahead and planning is crucial, but dwelling on the future beyond what's necessary puts you in the same mentally exhausting neural circuit as worrying. When you feel your attention drifting toward the end of a task, do like I did in Hell Week and pull it back to the present moment. Refocus on what you know and what you can influence *right now*.

The old saying "Keep your eyes on the prize" is often touted to hone focus and stir passion. However, fixating on the end goal isn't necessary to make progress or to maintain zeal. Your brain holds these objectives in its subconscious grasp. So once you set your goal, release it. You'll find yourself navigating toward it naturally as you devote your attention to the immediate tasks at hand. Tackle the journey one step at a time, crafting one meaningful DPO after another. This method conserves your cognitive and emotional reserves and sets the stage for successive waves of dopamine, each one propelling you smoothly to your next milestone.

CREATE MOTIVATION FOR MUNDANE TASKS

Those who subscribe to the grit myth often encounter an invisible barrier to the motivation they can harness for daily tasks, whether at home or at work. Seeing every task as a monolith to be powered through can lead to a dopamine deficit or, at the very least, a missed opportunity to utilize this drive-boosting chemical to its full potential.

Yet you can spark your own motivation by segmenting tasks into a succession of small, meaningful goals, no matter how routine they may seem. This tactic is especially handy for the everyday grind, which, depending on your environment and perspective, might feel monotonous.

Take, for instance, the creation of a slide deck—something you might do often and without much inherent challenge. It could seem dull or lackluster, or perhaps other factors are dampening your enthusiasm. What's the strategy? Divide it into bite-size, rewarding tasks. Get innovative with your horizon-setting. Introduce just enough challenge to each segment to yield personal satisfaction. This way, each minigoal achieved gives you a dopamine lift, fueling you toward the next goal, and when you finish the entire task, there's a dopamine surge waiting to be harnessed for your next endeavor.

The potential for any task is limitless, but it must resonate with you personally, so you need to be introspective and inventive with your capabilities. How might you dissect this hypothetical slide deck into a series of small achievements that feel significant to you?

For example, you could set a time challenge for researching each slide, establish new quality benchmarks for your slide content, or enhance your design skills by experimenting with the visual aspects of your presentation. The key is crafting milestones that are meaningful to you.

Adopting this approach more broadly might just transform the drudgery you once accepted as par for the course. Tasks become chances to amplify your drive rather than diminish it. Motivation is a complex beast, and while I won't claim a one-size-fits-all solution, crafting meaningful horizons could be a game changer. Tackle tasks by deconstructing them into these horizons, and you might just find yourself more motivated at the end than you were at the beginning.

Make this a regular practice, and you could well find yourself becoming more adept at maintaining or even enhancing your drive, especially when you need it the most.

KEY POINTS: CHAPTER 2

1. **Set Meaningful Horizons:** Set goals just beyond your comfort zone: not too big, not too small. This provides a sense of progress and achievement, which keeps you motivated and moving forward.

2. **Dopamine in Motivation:** Dopamine, often called the molecule of "pleasure" or "reward," also modulates drive and is why meaningful horizons are so important. The body doesn't make enough dopamine when goals are too daunting, and it makes too little when goals are too modest. Set meaningful horizons, and you'll get a series of dopamine rewards that you can use to advance to subsequent horizons.

3. **Let Go of the End Goal:** The adage "Keep your eye on the prize" can sometimes be counterproductive. Fixating too much on the end point can create stress and drain your motivation. Instead, concentrate on what you can manage in the present.

4. **Horizons for Teams:** The sense of achievement from collaborating and navigating unique experiences together is inherently rewarding and can lead to significant dopamine spikes, propelling teams toward

remarkable performance. Build on this reward by setting meaningful goals for the team as a whole. More about this in chapter 7.

CHAPTER 3

STAY COOL

Tools to Modulate Autonomic Arousal

In a world often fixated on the negative aspects of stress, few explore the innate faculties our physiology offers to control autonomic arousal. Yet Masters of Uncertainty, while navigating the high seas of extreme conditions, have been tapping into this ability for eons.

Masters of Uncertainty know that even while the substance of thoughts amid ambiguity is pivotal for success, the brain is inextricably linked to a broader nervous system, intertwined with the body's symphony. They stay attuned to the physiological reactions that accompany uncertainty and challenge because they understand viscerally that modulating the body modulates the mind.

Modern-day scientists like my friend and colleague Dr. Andrew Huberman (with whom I've had the honor of collaborating on the constructs of Duration, Pathway, and Outcome) are subjecting these ancient practices to the crucible of science. The evidence is compelling: we possess the ability to modulate autonomic arousal. We can harness it to elevate performance and maintain composure in the midst of challenge, uncertainty, and stress.

AUTONOMIC AROUSAL: THE BODY'S NATURAL ACCELERANT

Autonomic arousal is the body's natural boost. It ignites a cascade of biochemical changes (such as pumping adrenaline and cortisol into the blood) to energize us when facing a challenge or threat. This stimulating response can be incredibly beneficial, offering surges of energy and heightened alertness that enhance both physical readiness and mental sharpness.

However, there's a threshold. If these levels climb without restraint, or if you start to lose your grip on the present, you may teeter toward panic. Overstimulation can lead you to impulsive decisions or lackluster performance, disrupting your ability to move horizons and progress toward your goals. It's essential to remain connected with your body's signals and their interplay with your mind and performance. To function at your best, find and maintain the ideal level of autonomic arousal for each circumstance.

The neurology that underpins this balance is an interplay between two major circuits in the brain. The frontal lobe is the part of the brain responsible for rational decision-making; it's the key part that contemplates then executes carefully considered plans. It evolved relatively recently and is therefore often referred to as the "modern brain." The limbic system is the part of the brain that handles emotional and instinctual responses. It is ancient and buried deeper in the physical structure of the brain, more closely aligned with our animal past. It is often referred to as the "lizard brain." As environments become steeped in uncertainty and autonomic arousal climbs, the frontal lobe begins to yield to the limbic system. In simplified terms, the modern brain yields to the ancient, instinctive lizard brain as it rises up to protect you with survival instinct.

If this shift goes unchecked, it can spiral into what's known as autonomic overload (or "amygdala hijack," as the amygdala plays a key role in initiating autonomic arousal): actions become *reflexive* rather than *reflective*. The limbic system's instinctive response is invaluable in the face of immediate, life-threatening dangers, like jumping out of the way of an oncoming train, but it's typically unhelpful in the complex uncertainties of contemporary life. Reacting purely on emotion can lead to actions that may exacerbate the situation rather than resolve it.

The primary purpose of the embodied practices I offer in this chapter is to regulate your physiological state to decrease autonomic arousal. This is the common need most of the time, as uncertainty and stress are pervasive. Learn to decrease autonomic arousal, and you can not only reduce the discomfort of stress but also reengage the frontal lobe. You can more easily return to a state of making conscious, rational decisions. Calm your body, and you calm your mind.

There are also times when you need the opposite: you need *more* autonomic arousal, a boost of energy or alertness. You don't need to calm down but rather to ramp up. You can intentionally dial *up* your autonomic arousal with embodied practices. Energize your body, and you energize your mind.

Masters of Uncertainty excel in this modulation: they skillfully adjust their internal mechanisms to fine-tune autonomic arousal, achieving the ideal level for any given circumstance. You can too. In the following section, I present some visual and respiratory techniques to help you gain greater mastery over your mental and physical states, empowering you to navigate uncertainty and reach your goals. These tools are designed to give you control over your body's responses, helping you navigate through various states of arousal and maintain optimal performance.

VISUAL TOOLS

Vision is our primary means of engaging with the world. A staggering 40 percent of the brain is devoted to the visual system. This has significant, if little-known, implications for autonomic arousal: it is the most potent sense for influencing our physiology.

The visual system operates in two primary modes: focused and panoramic vision. Focused vision is akin to the intense, targeted gaze of a hunting cheetah, designed to zero in on and pursue prey. Panoramic vision is like the broad, encompassing gaze of a cow surveying a field, taking in a wide expanse to maintain awareness of its surroundings. We humans are uniquely equipped to switch between these two visual modes. Focused vision kicks in when you're deeply engaged in tasks like reading or playing sports. Panoramic vision is what you use when a broad awareness of the environment is more beneficial, such as when driving or walking in nature. The key point is that these two visual modes are intimately linked with autonomic arousal.

When a threat looms and autonomic arousal begins to rise, focused vision activates, and vision tends to narrow. This natural response heightens the ability to concentrate on the critical circumstance demanding attention. In extreme cases, this can lead to "tunnel vision," where perception is limited to the threat itself, and all else falls away. It's obvious that this intense focus is crucial in high-stakes situations that require immediate action and rapid decision-making, like when on a Navy SEAL mission or facing a serious emergency. However, it's also present in everyday scenarios that, while less dramatic, still trigger a concentrated response, such as a difficult meeting, a personal argument, or a minor mishap.

But here's the cool part: we can consciously influence this response. By intentionally shifting from focused to panoramic vision, we can dial back autonomic arousal. Panoramic vision decreases brain stimulation and neural activity, aiding the frontal lobe in regaining dominance. This shift allows for more thoughtful deliberation, a calming of the mind, and a return to a state of balance throughout both mind and body.

Another fascinating aspect of these visual modes is that they not only affect how we see but also affect our perception of time. With focused vision, we experience what could be described as a "soda straw" view of the world: limited in scope, yet incredibly detailed. The brain is in overdrive and processes time in incredibly fine slices: second by second, or even millisecond by millisecond. This intense processing can be draining and, paradoxically, make time seem to stretch out endlessly. That's why, in moments of acute focus, like in a car accident, time appears to move in slow motion. With the brain operating at such a rapid clip, there's little room for the delays of conscious decision-making.

Panoramic vision, conversely, utilizes a more relaxed set of neural pathways. These pathways are designed for multitasking and broader environmental awareness. Time is sliced more generously, seeming to accelerate. Consider a day spent on the beach: often it feels like the hours simply "fly by." This mode implies a brain state that is loose and at ease, allowing conscious decision-making to be fully accessible and unhindered.

FOCUSED AND PANORAMIC VISION

The goal is to consciously use your vision to help induce the level of arousal needed at any given moment. You can heighten autonomic arousal and its focus-enhancing benefits by deliberately using focused vision. Conversely, you can lower autonomic arousal to facilitate more thoughtful, conscious decision-making by switching to panoramic vision.

When it comes to sharpening focus, the principle is quite straightforward: direct your attention to the task at hand. While this may be challenging for some, and maintaining that focus can sometimes be even more difficult, there are strategies to assist you. Perhaps the most critical is the intentional elimination of distractions. These can come from various sources, but for many of us, the primary culprit is the smartphone. Even the smallest ping or vibration can disrupt mental processing, so it's imperative to remove such interruptions. For example, when public speaking, I often choose to set my phone somewhere I can't access it, far away from my person. The slightest vibration could pull me out of my zone of focused attention, disrupting my autonomic arousal "sweet spot."

When it comes to reducing autonomic arousal, particularly when facing uncertainty or adapting to changing environments, panoramic vision is invaluable. This can be achieved through a technique called "soft gaze."

To practice soft gaze: Choose an object in your environment—a wall, a window, or a tree. Focus on it, then gently relax your eyes. Begin to include the periphery in your vision. Slowly, you'll become aware of your 180-degree field of vision without actively focusing on anything specific. Typically if you maintain this for a couple of minutes, you'll likely notice a calming effect. This is the sign that your autonomic arousal is diminishing, paving the way for clearer, more conscious thinking.

Panoramic vision has been a staple for me, especially when confronting nerves. To calm myself before jumping out of a perfectly good airplane during my time in the SEALs, I'd gaze out at the horizon from the plane, inviting a wider view. Once out of the Navy, and during my initial forays into public speaking, I used it to lessen my anxiety on stage, focusing not on the audience directly but on the space around them. Panoramic vision has been a consistent technique in my repertoire for maintaining calm in nerve-inducing scenarios.

EMDR FOR DECREASING AUTONOMIC AROUSAL

EMDR stands for eye movement desensitization and reprocessing, a technique widely recognized in the realm of mental health therapy.

The method itself is quite simple: an object, such as your finger, is moved from side to side in front of your eyes. You hold your head steady and follow its lateral movement with your eyes alone. This eye movement technique has been proven to lower autonomic arousal, fostering both stress reduction and relaxation. It's also an effective tool for trauma therapy because it taps into the brain's associative links between sensory input and negative memories.

The lateral movements encourage the brain to enter a state of relaxation, which in turn aids in reprocessing difficult memories without activating a stressed autonomic response. (Therapeutically, it's always facilitated by a trained therapist.) EMDR has gained fame for its success in treating post-traumatic stress disorder and is now being applied to a broader spectrum of issues.

For those looking to master uncertainty, the lateral eye movements used in EMDR can help to reduce autonomic arousal. While the science and formal therapeutic applications of EMDR are relatively modern developments, the underlying principle of this technique is quite old—it is, for example, why hypnotists have long used the image of a pendulum to induce relaxation and suggestibility in their subjects.

To use EMDR techniques for reducing autonomic arousal, here's a simple method to try: Locate a quiet spot where you can sit or stand undisturbed for a short time. Hold up one or two fingers—typically the index and middle—about half an arm's length from your face. Keep your head stationary, and focus on your fingers. Sweep your fingers from left to right, extending to a forty-five-degree angle on either side. Follow the movement solely with your eyes, not your head. Continue this for thirty seconds to a minute. You'll likely notice a sense of relaxation and a clearing of your thoughts as you do this.

What's particularly beneficial about these visual techniques is their versatility; they can be employed practically anytime, anywhere. While EMDR might be better suited for a private space (since tracking your finger movements might attract some curious looks if you're in a public setting), the underlying principle of these various visual techniques is the same, and they are effective tools for managing autonomic arousal levels.

RESPIRATORY TOOLS

Breath work is being increasingly recognized for its benefits. Yet many remain unaware of the true possibilities for modulation it brings, and among those who are aware, it is unfortunately common to forget it in times of stress or challenge.

The respiratory system holds a powerful influence over

autonomic arousal and can be a significant tool not just in moments of acute uncertainty but also in everyday life. Research conducted has recently shown that the parts of the brain stem responsible for regulating voluntary breathing also interact with the areas that govern emotion. This means that ancient techniques practiced by Masters of Uncertainty now have scientific backing: breathing and the mind are interconnected. By consciously controlling your breath, you can regulate both your physiology and your mental state.

OXYGEN-DOMINATED (INHALE-EMPHASIZED) BREATHING

In chapter 1, I explained how stress and uncertainty sometimes lead to procrastination—a passive loss of time and potential solutions as you drift in a haze of distraction and stress. However, those adept at navigating uncertainty know that action equates to success.

Sometimes what you need is to summon enough energy and sharpness to start crafting DPOs and advancing horizons, no matter how modest the steps may be. (Note: There are times when inaction is the strategic choice, but it should be a deliberate decision. Even in choosing to do nothing, a DPO and horizon can be established around that choice.) Oxygen-dominated breathing techniques are a potent means to enhance alertness and autonomic arousal. They can propel you into a state ready for action.

One method is *cyclic hyperventilation*. This involves a deep inhale through the nose immediately followed by a deep exhale (active or passive) through the mouth. Repeat this pattern twenty-five times, then fully exhale until your lungs are empty, and then hold at the bottom for about fifteen seconds. This kind of breathing activates the sympathetic nervous system, thereby boosting alertness and energy.

Another technique is *Kapalabhati Pranayama,* also known as the Breath of Fire. This ancient yogic practice consists of natural, passive inhales and short, forceful exhales. Inhale through your nose, feeling your belly expand as you do so. Without pausing, exhale forcefully through your nose while contracting your abdominal muscles. Keep your inhales and exhales equal in length. Repeat several times for about thirty seconds and try speeding up your inhales and exhales as you go. This swiftly oxygenates the blood, heightening energy and mental focus.

These oxygen-rich breathing practices come with a host of benefits: they energize the body for optimal cellular function, balance blood pH levels, sharpen mental focus, and help regulate the nervous system. They're versatile tools, ready to be used whenever you need to elevate autonomic arousal.

CO_2 BLOWOUT (EXHALE-EMPHASIZED) BREATHING

In most situations fraught with challenge or uncertainty, it's quite normal for autonomic arousal to escalate, sometimes sharply. As discussed throughout this book, if this surge isn't managed, it can significantly diminish your capacity for conscious, rational decision-making, which is essential for formulating DPOs and moving horizons. But what actually happens in the body to trigger such stress and anxiety?

A common misconception is that the urge to breathe, whether you're underwater or holding your breath on land, is due to a lack of oxygen. In reality, it's the accumulation of CO_2 that causes discomfort. This reveals an intriguing aspect of our physiology: the buildup of CO_2 is linked to autonomic arousal. Fortunately, you can exploit this connection by reversing the process. Reduce CO_2 levels, and you calm autonomic arousal.

The physiological sigh is one such method. This is a simple and effective breathing technique that involves two inhales through the nose, followed by a longer, slow exhale through the mouth. Try inhaling once through your nose, filling your lungs. At the top, take a second, quicker inhale to almost "top off" your lung capacity. Then conduct an extended exhale through the mouth. Repeat this between five and ten times, and you will feel noticeably calmer and more relaxed.

This pattern aids in fully inflating the lungs and then

expelling air to stimulate relaxation. It's particularly useful for stress reduction, as it helps balance the sympathetic nervous system (stress response) and parasympathetic nervous system (relaxation response), leading to decreased stress levels and improved mood. Cyclic sighing can be easily integrated into daily life, offering a quick method to manage stress and anxiety in various situations.

Another approach is the 4-7-8 breathing technique crafted by Dr. Andrew Weil. This simple yet powerful practice involves inhaling through the nose for four seconds, holding that breath for seven seconds, and exhaling thoroughly through the mouth for eight seconds. This rhythm serves as a natural sedative for the nervous system, reducing stress and anxiety.

Both of these methods are tremendously beneficial for handling stress, mitigating anxiety, and decreasing autonomic arousal, allowing you to remain composed and ready to navigate through uncertainty.

BOX BREATHING

At times, you may find yourself in the ideal state of autonomic arousal, perfectly attuned to your environment and its demands. However, changes around you can threaten to disrupt this balance. Navy SEALs employ a technique known as box breathing to counteract this. Picture your breath moving along the edges of a square box, with each side representing a step:

inhale for five seconds, hold for five seconds, exhale for five seconds, and hold again for five seconds.

This method is effective in maintaining autonomic stability amid stress because it syncs breath with a balanced in-and-out pattern. Equal parts inhalation and exhalation facilitate a harmonious balance of oxygen and CO_2 in the blood. Box breathing preserves this equilibrium. In doing so, it supports mental clarity and physiological readiness, enabling you to navigate through stressful times without losing your stride.

KEY POINTS: CHAPTER 3

1. **Apply these techniques on an ad hoc basis or alongside other activities:** Say you're in the midst of a stressful workday and suddenly remember that deep breathing can help you maintain composure. You can subtly adjust your breathing while continuing with your tasks, such as by breathing deeply while reading a document or engaging panoramic vision by looking out a window during a phone call. If it could be helpful for you to be reminded of such techniques, try placing a sticky note in a frequent line of sight—on your computer, a mirror, or the steering wheel of your car—as a prompt to breathe or to use vision effectively as needed.

2. **Set horizons to implement these techniques on their own:** Sometimes the best way to move toward a goal is to take some extra time to create the best physiological and mental setup you can. So rather than breathing absentmindedly while engaged in another task, carve out a specific time to focus solely on your breathing or vision practice. Allocating time to intentionally modulate autonomic arousal allows for a deeper, more comprehensive approach. Concentrate fully on these regulatory practices, and you not only enhance their immediate benefits but also set yourself up for success in subsequent activities. By achieving the ideal state of arousal, you prime yourself for effective action.

3. **Use these techniques to master uncertainty:** In the thick of profound uncertainty, stress, and challenge, success hinges on your ability to consciously craft DPOs and set horizons. This is only possible with an engaged frontal lobe, unhindered flow, and empowerment of the brain's decision-making faculties. In moments when uncertainty nudges you toward panic or overwhelm, employ these techniques to dial up or dial back the arousal, activate your conscious thinking, and strategically navigate your way through.

PART II

MASTERING YOUR SELF

In part I, we explored the innate abilities we all share. You discovered how humans naturally move horizons, keep going, and regulate arousal in pursuit of goals regardless of the challenges faced.

Part II gets into the next three steps of the Mastering Uncertainty Method by shifting the focus to the natural elements that define your personal abilities: the unique aspects of your being that shape your performance in uncertain situations. These include your attributes, identities, and objectives.

Your attributes are your elemental "hows": the distinctive

ways you approach tasks. Your identities are your elemental "whats": the unique principles guiding your actions in the face of uncertainty, challenge, and stress. Your objectives are your "whys": your purposes made concrete, driving you toward your goals.

Masters of Uncertainty thrive on knowledge. Moving horizons involves understanding the present circumstances, enabling strategic decisions. However, this external knowledge is only part of the equation. You also need internal knowledge—self-awareness about who you are. You must understand your hows, whats, and whys.

By clarifying these fundamental aspects of your self, you can leverage this insight to your advantage. These revelations are not just transformative for your personal life; they also form the bedrock of high-performing teams. When a team is clear on its attributes, identity, and objectives, it can effectively implement dynamic subordination, a leadership model that fosters trust, agility, endurance, and exceptional performance.

CHAPTER 4

ATTRIBUTES

Innate Performance Drivers

Have you ever seen the movie Cars?

Every character is a different type of vehicle. There are sleek Ferraris, robust SUVs, rugged Jeeps—each with their own set of capabilities. There's no hierarchy, no better or worse. The cars are simply diverse, with each better suited to its own terrain. This is key to their success.

Imagine a Ferrari struggling to climb up a bumpy, off-road track. It's a mismatch. The Ferrari isn't at fault; it's just not designed for that environment. Conversely, a Jeep on a racetrack would be equally out of place because it's not designed for the necessary turns and speed. When you watch the movie, you naturally understand this and don't judge the vehicles. They each excel in the right setting.

Cars communicates a simple and powerful truth, one as

vital for adults as it is for children: we all have a set of innate strengths, and each person's is unique. It's not better or worse. Just unique. True success doesn't come from lamenting the abilities you lack but from recognizing and utilizing the ones you possess. While it's beneficial to learn and to grow, it's most efficient to play to your strengths. A Jeep will never corner like a Ferrari, no matter the effort. You're much more likely to succeed if you work to become the finest Jeep rather than an imitation Ferrari.

Optimal performance doesn't call for an overhaul, just a deeper self-understanding. Identify your "model," embrace it, and drive forward using that knowledge. This is the secret not only to top performance but also to mastering the unpredictable twists and turns of life.

TRUE PERFORMANCE INDICATORS

In 1943, Navy Lieutenant Draper Kauffman was tapped to assemble a group of soldiers who could swim ahead and clear the way for Allied Forces on D-Day. His initial team, the Naval Combat Demolition Unit, was the very first version of today's US Navy SEALs. Kauffman had a keen eye for the essential: he understood that being a strong swimmer who could sneak across the beach wasn't enough for his recruits. He needed men who could think on their feet. Men who could adapt and flex as fast as the environment did. Men who had the ability to be aware of multiple aspects of their surroundings, work together as a team, and learn new things quickly—and do so while under unfathomable stress.

Kauffman was hunting for insight into these men that didn't yet exist in any formalized system. He dug deeper to those intrinsic attributes that define a person's core—the fundamental qualities that dictate how each of us engages with the world, solves problems, and makes decisions. When it became my job to figure out precisely what determines the kinds of high performance we see in Navy SEALs, I began intensively studying and categorizing these attributes. They operate like the underlying code of an app: invisible yet crucial drivers of functionality. They are not our actions but rather the forces that shape and direct these actions. In the most testing times, these attributes emerge starkly, revealing our most elemental selves.

Every individual is endowed with some amount of each of the forty-one attributes, creating a unique constellation of characteristics that is as personal as a fingerprint. Imagine a control panel with forty-one dimmers, each set to a distinct level, shaping an individual's attribute profile. This profile typically bears similarities within professions, much like the inherent designs of the characters in *Cars*. Different attributes determine aptitude for different tasks and terrains. This diversity in our natural makeup is what predicates our distinct capabilities and paths in work and life.

IDENTIFY YOUR ATTRIBUTES

Attributes aren't cryptic. If you haven't learned yours yet, it's only because you haven't been able to articulate them.

First, learn about the range of classifications as outlined in my first book, *The Attributes: 25 Hidden Drivers of Optimal Performance*. While in the book I discuss the first twenty-five, there are, in fact, forty-one, broken into nine categories:

1. **Grit:** Courage, Perseverance, Adaptability, Resilience.
2. **Mental Acuity:** Situational Awareness, Compartmentalization, Task Switching, Learnability, Discernment.
3. **Drive:** Self-Efficacy, Narcissism, Competitiveness, Discipline.
4. **Commitment:** Persistence, Tenacity, Confidence, Optimism, Patience.
5. **Vision:** Creativity, Innovativeness, Cunning, Open-Mindedness, Curiosity.
6. **Social Intelligence:** Humor, Charisma, Influence, Extroversion, Emotional Intelligence.
7. **Service:** Empathy, Compassion, Caring, Generosity, Selflessness.
8. **Leadership:** Authenticity, Decisiveness, Accountability.
9. **Teamability:** Integrity, Conscientiousness, Humility, Collaborative, Insouciance.

Then figure out where you stand. The best method is the assessment tool on our website (visit **hub.theattributes.com**), which provides a breakdown of your attribute profile, strengths, and weaknesses.

Embarking on a journey of self-discovery, you can also uncover your attributes by reflecting on how you've navigated life's more turbulent waters. Those moments in your past that brimmed over with stress or challenge are where your attributes are most discernible. Ask yourself: Which attributes shone through, and which faltered? Seek insight from friends or colleagues for a balanced view. Attributes lie at the very core of performance in all aspects of life, but especially during stress, challenge, and uncertainty. Take time to figure out where you sit with each one and the implications for your natural strengths and weaknesses. This will help provide a solid understanding of what you need to do to excel amid challenge and uncertainty.

DEVELOP YOUR ATTRIBUTES

Is it possible to cultivate your attributes? To an extent. Attributes aren't immutable, yet they are deeply rooted. They are a result of the interplay of genetic makeup and formative experiences—a blend of nature and nurture that is very deeply habituated, nearly hardwired. They have gradually shifted over the course of your life, influenced by your experiences.

Presently, they exist at a specific intensity, somewhat steadfast. However, with focused effort, persistent practice, and time, they can evolve.

The excellent news is that while you *can* develop your attributes (see *The Attributes* for more on how), that's not what you need to focus on for optimal performance. What you need is to know what you're working with: What is your attribute profile? How much of each attribute do you possess? This illuminates your unique strengths and weaknesses. Gain this knowledge, and you and any team you're on gain a crucial leg up in deciding what steps to take—that is, in moving horizons—through the uncertain conditions of business and life.

LEVERAGE YOUR ATTRIBUTES TO NAVIGATE UNCERTAINTY

Your attribute profile is a powerful tool. The key is not to judge but to effectively utilize what you've got. Acknowledge what you're good at and what you're not, then strategize accordingly.

When facing new ventures or working with others, your attributes should be front and center. Use your strengths to your advantage, and find ways to counterbalance your weaknesses.

For example, if you're abundant in patience, you'll naturally excel in situations that require a calm and persistent approach, like tasks that are slow-moving or necessitate waiting. When speed is of the essence, you may be served by reaching out to less patient friends or colleagues for advice. Conversely, if you lack patience (neither patience or impatience is better or worse), you will likely benefit from unleashing your natural speed in scenarios that demand quick decisions or prompt actions. When waiting is necessary, you will want to be aware of your inclination to rush; choose actions (set horizons) accordingly. Take measures to compensate, such as scheduling periodic pauses or following the lead of others who are more patient. Be aware of both yourself and your environment, and take steps to adjust your approach.

In your professional life, aim for roles that let your attributes shine. Every team role has an ideal attribute match. Being a surgeon requires more compartmentalization than empathy, for example, whereas for a family practitioner, it's the reverse. Excelling in sales requires being high on adaptability, influence, and perseverance. When your attributes align with your responsibilities, you'll experience a flow that feels like you're on the right track, enhancing both your satisfaction and performance.

Should you find yourself dissatisfied in a role, consider that it might be a matter of attribute mismatch. Engage in discussions about better-fitting opportunities. And if you must operate in less-than-ideal conditions, find ways to work with your attributes, such as asking for help or allowing more time to complete tasks. This approach will help you navigate through your responsibilities more effectively.

ATTRIBUTES FOR TEAMS

Attributes are just as vital to a team's performance as they are to an individual. Instead of focusing solely on skills, it's more effective to align team members' roles with their inherent attributes. Optimal job satisfaction and performance spring from this alignment. I explain how to craft high-performing teams using attribute profiles in chapter 9.

Attributes also play a crucial role in team success amid uncertainty. Teams that leverage an understanding of each member's attributes for dynamic subordination and role adaptation thrive amid the unpredictable conditions of business. Knowing the strengths and weaknesses within the team fosters both a fluid exchange of roles and also trust in leadership capabilities, which I discuss in detail in chapter 7.

KEY POINTS: CHAPTER 4

1. **Leverage Innate Strengths for Optimal Performance:** Individuals have unique strengths that determine their optimal environments—success comes from recognizing and utilizing these inherent strengths rather than lamenting what one lacks. Understanding your "model" and playing to your strengths is key to achieving top performance and navigating life's unpredictability.

2. **Attributes as Core Performance Indicators:** Attributes are intrinsic qualities that dictate how we engage with the world, solve problems, and make decisions, much like the underlying code of an app. Attributes are invisible yet crucial drivers of functionality, especially in high-stress situations.

3. **Identifying and Assessing Attributes:** Attributes are not cryptic but can be articulated and assessed. Understanding your attribute profile through assessments and self-reflection helps identify natural strengths and weaknesses, providing a foundation for personal and professional growth.

4. **Developing and Utilizing Attributes:** While attributes are deeply rooted, they can be developed with focused effort and practice. However, optimal performance comes from understanding and leveraging your current attribute profile. In team settings, focusing on attributes rather than just skills fosters better role adaptation, trust, and overall team success, especially under uncertain conditions.

CHAPTER 5

IDENTITIES

The Subconscious Source of Action

On November 17, 2012, José Salvador Alvarenga and Ezequiel Córdoba embarked on what they expected to be a brief thirty-six-hour expedition into open seas for commercial fishing. But mere hours into the voyage, a ferocious storm unexpectedly coalesced on their path. It proceeded to aggressively pummel their modest vessel for five days.

When skies eventually cleared, they found themselves without an engine, the majority of their fishing equipment, radio contact, or any form of sail or paddles. They were aimlessly adrift, completely at the mercy of the mercurial ocean.

Weeks turned into months. They ran out of food and began to survive solely on sea life—turtles, fish, and jellyfish—that they somehow managed to ensnare with their hands. After four grueling months, desolation took its toll on Córdoba, and he succumbed to illness and despair. Alvarenga, now solitary, persisted in the face of total isolation. He drifted for an additional nine months before finally drifting close enough to an island, where he found salvation.

Throughout these 438 days, Alvarenga was besieged by depression, his thoughts flirting with suicide. Yet one powerful thought acted as a beacon of meaning and hope through this darkness: "I am a Christian."

In English, the phrase "I am" possesses an extraordinary potency. It is the precursor to a self-fulfilling prophecy. It shapes your whole focus and, by extension, your reality. Those two words and whatever follow are, in essence, your identity.

The problem for most is misinterpreting or undervaluing these words, leading to an inner conflict about who they are. For every person, what follows after the words "I am" is a complex tapestry, woven from various values, ideals, and subconscious archetypes that lie at the core. Make no mistake, however: these intrinsic elements make up your identity (or identities), and they exert an undeniable sway over your decisions and actions in the face of uncertainty.

Moving horizons amid uncertainty demands that we recognize the identities that propel us toward certain actions. To understand these identities allows you to know what drives you in times of uncertainty and challenge. Getting clear on who you are at your core means you can use this information to your advantage. You can harness facets of your identity that serve you while steering clear of ones that may lead you astray. In the same way you can rely on or compensate for various attributes to increase chances of success, you can also rely on or compensate for various aspects of your identity to increase chances of success. Remain rooted in your essence and utilize the familiar to steer through the unknown. This will propel you to the outcomes you desire.

THE RULES AND BIASES YOU FOLLOW

In the preceding chapter, I delineated the attributes as the essential code sculpting your behavioral patterns: they are your fundamental *hows*. Your identity—or *identities*—define your fundamental *whats*. They furnish you with the instinctual guidelines and predispositions you adhere to amid uncertainty.

Your few core identities play a pivotal role in what you do in any scenario. In the throes of profound uncertainty, they often emerge as the sole determinants. Deep uncertainty, challenge, and stress often divest us of more surface-level elements of who we are—such as our ideals, habits, preferences, or even personality, revealing the core identities that lie beneath. One consequence (or benefit), though, is that when absent of Duration, Pathway, and Outcome, actions do not always align with aspirations. Instead, they end up guided by deep-seated, subconscious conceptions of self.

We are all mosaics of various identities. Numerous "I ams" coalesce to constitute our unique beings. Some identities are more central than others. A multitude of identities originate from familial bonds: mother, father, uncle, sister. Some stem from specific ideological or political affiliations: Muslim, Christian, atheist, Democrat, Republican. Others are defined by profession: lawyer, doctor, teacher, soldier. Some are aligned with particular causes: environmentalist, socialist, Libertarian. And some are born out of sheer affinities: Harley-Davidson aficionado, Taylor Swift groupie, Boston Red Sox fan.

Indeed, we accumulate diverse identities as we journey through life. For instance, some of my identities are (or have been) lacrosse player, Purdue University grad, Navy SEAL, husband, father, motorcycle enthusiast, and Metallica fan.

All such identities, each with their own set of rules and biases delineating their essence, have the propensity to mold behavior. As creatures of society, the roles and conducts of our various identities jostle to exert their influence on us. They push to the fore or fall back, depending on the context, driving us either to assimilate into a group or to distinguish ourselves from it (an identity in itself: the rebel). The most dominant of your myriad identities are interwoven throughout your entire psyche, reaching into the subconscious, operating always from your core. Consequently, your actions are profoundly influenced by your convictions regarding the rules and norms of your few most core identities—and especially in uncertainty, when your raw self is at the helm.

For José Salvador Alvarenga, a core tenet of his Christian identity—that taking one's own life is a sin and that he bore the responsibility to strive for survival—was the driving force behind his actions at a fundamental level. This tenet was a *belief*, but the power of it—the reason it could sustain him through such dark times—was how deeply it was embedded in his identity as a Christian. Alvarenga's core identity fueled his allegiance to this tenet through a time of profound uncertainty, in the stark absence of Duration, Pathway, and Outcome.

Like Alvarenga, our identities propel our behavior: always, for better or worse, and particularly when we face uncertainty, challenge, and stress. The old wisdom bears true: a person's authentic essence is revealed not necessarily by what they say but by what they do. Our essence is our deeds.

DISCOVER YOUR PRIMARY IDENTITIES

Explore your identities diligently. If you do not, you risk remaining oblivious to some of the reasons behind your performance. You may act only on instinct and miss opportunities to chart a more strategic path.

For me, the roles of "husband and father," "Navy SEAL," and "author" are not merely titles but foundational aspects of my identity. Out of the three, however, it is as a "husband and father" that I find my most instinctive rules and biases, the ones that dictate the majority of my actions and decisions. This is the lens through which I predominantly view the world, the identity that shapes my reality in most situations. Yet the salience of any individual identity is not set in stone. When I was leading a SEAL troop in the war zone, it was the "Navy SEAL" identity whose rules and biases became priority.

It is your primary identities, the ones that resonate most deeply within, that pilot your actions and behaviors when at your most raw. Consequently, mapping out the terrain of your identities is an important exercise. Take a moment to sit with pen and paper, and write "I am ________" several times. Do not hesitate to repeat this as many times as required. Explore the breadth of potential identities. Even identities that seem peripheral may play a role in shaping your behavior. Consider family relationships, community roles, various group roles, your profession, your causes, your hobbies, and your likes and dislikes. ("I am a Nickelback hater" is an identity that will shape at least some of your biases!)

To discern which identities take precedence, reflect upon times when you've faced adversity or when the stakes were high. Such moments are revelatory flashpoints, stripping back the layers to reveal your most primary sense of self. It's a process that requires not just introspection but transparency, weighing the self as you perceive it against the self as it truly is.

Invite those you trust into this journey of self-discovery. Share your insights; welcome their observations. They likely have a perspective on your identity that you've missed. Others have a vantage point that can almost always illuminate parts of yourself you can't see.

Embrace this exercise without self-criticism. Identities are not inherently virtuous or flawed; they are simply the prisms through which we engage with the world. Even an identity you may perceive as negative, such as "I'm a smoker," once recognized, can be reevaluated and redefined. Mastering the uncertainties of life does not require reinvention but rather a profound understanding of the identities you carry. Knowledge, in this sense, is the prelude to transformation.

LEVERAGE YOUR KNOWLEDGE OF IDENTITY

In uncertainty, awareness of the inherent rules and biases that guide your actions can afford crucial insight. Embrace moments where you can pause and reflect, and ask yourself: What might you be subconsciously exaggerating or neglecting based on your self-perceptions? For me, my "Navy SEAL" identity can skew my expectations of others, sometimes unrealistically.

A great example is the way Navy SEALs view time and punctuality. For most civilians, the standard rule is, "Anytime between start time and fifteen minutes is fine." In the regular military, it's, "If you are not fifteen minutes early, you are late." For Navy SEALs, it's, "Plus or minus thirty seconds." In the Navy SEAL world, being too early is just as bad as being too late. Whatever time is given, the rule of punctuality means that you'll be there at *that* time, plus or minus thirty seconds. Precision matters.

In day-to-day interactions beyond the regimented life of a SEAL, I've learned to moderate this rigid rule of punctuality. I've intentionally adapted to the more lax approach of those not bound by the same strict code. At the same time, when immersed in uncertainty, challenge, and stress, I can default back to the more deeply habituated way of being strict with punctuality and expecting others to do the same. I *know* this about myself, and I use this awareness to check my expectations and behavior—and the horizons I set—as best I can.

This adjustment is emblematic of the broader necessity to look beyond instinctive rules. Pause and evaluate your instinct. Do not just acknowledge but actively seek out a spectrum of actions that diverge from your gut reaction. If cool reflection reveals that your instinct truly is the optimal path, then commit to it, moving your horizons with precision and intent. If it isn't, hold your instinct in check while you consider other options. Seek, if possible, perspective or help from others who have different identities. Make space for yourself to consider alternative strategies or to take things slower. Often, simply committing to slowing down while you set horizons can help you see beyond the instincts you carry. Adjust your horizons by creating a Duration, Pathway, and Outcome accordingly.

Finally, there may be times when leaning on an identity (and the actions that come with it) is exactly what is needed in the moment. Where it's necessary to say, "As a parent, what is the appropriate action in this moment?" Or, as was the case for me on occasion, "As a Navy SEAL, what should I do right now?" These are ways that we can leverage our identity for action—even when we may be unclear as to what action to take. Our identities can serve as guideposts—much like they did for Alvarenga in some of his darkest moments.

IDENTITIES FOR TEAMS

The potency of a collective identity within a team is immeasurable. At its essence, a team is a manifestation of a shared identity—a confluence of individuals aligned toward a singular purpose or objective. This alignment isn't just about the common goal. It's a synergy of values and a unison of intent, where each member's actions are harmonized by shared principles and expectations. These are the tacit rules and conditions that stem from the "I ams" of the group identity.

When navigating uncertainty, it's paramount that each team member's personal identity resonates with the group identity. The congruence of these identities ensures that, even when pressed to the edge, each individual's actions will serve the team's collective good, forging a trust that every member will act in concert with the team's core values.

Teams that excel, and especially those that deftly handle uncertainty, do not just share but consciously reinforce their collective identity. They explicitly articulate their shared values and the behaviors that embody these values: the rules and conditions that anchor all to the team's mission. To excel, focus on establishing your team's ethos and ensure that each member not only understands but is also empowered by this collective identity.

I explain the nuances of building a robust team identity and how to leverage it to create a thriving, high-performing team culture in chapter 9.

KEY POINTS: CHAPTER 5

1. **Identities and Their Influence:** Identities play a pivotal role in guiding behavior, especially in uncertainty. These identities furnish instinctual guidelines and predispositions, influencing actions at a fundamental level. We are mosaics of various identities (familial roles, ideological affiliations, professions, personal interests, and more), each molding behavior in different contexts. In deep uncertainty, core identities emerge as the sole determinants of actions.

2. **Discovering and Embracing Primary Identities:** Writing "I am ________" statements helps to uncover the identities that most influence behavior. Embrace this exercise without self-criticism, as identities are prisms through which we engage with the world.

3. **Leveraging Identity for Strategic Action:** Awareness of the inherent rules and biases guiding actions offers crucial insights, especially in uncertainty. Reflect on how self-perceptions might skew behavior and adjust accordingly. Evaluate instincts and consider alternative actions, seeking perspectives from others with different identities.

4. **Using Identity as a Guide in Critical Moments:** In times of uncertainty, relying on core identities can guide actions effectively. Asking questions like, "As a parent, what is the appropriate action?" leverages identity for decision-making. Identities can serve as guideposts, providing direction and purpose when clarity is needed.

CHAPTER 6

OBJECTIVES

Turn Purpose into Concrete Goals

IMAGINE A SEVENTEEN-YEAR-OLD KID with a burning desire to serve and protect others as a warrior. He knows his purpose: his "why."

But he's not drawn to the regular military. He wants something unique, challenging, and different—something that will set him apart.

Then he discovers an elite special operations unit he'd never heard of before. This team performs extraordinary feats: parachuting from tens of thousands of feet, diving stealthily into enemy harbors to disable ships, and rescuing hostages from dangerous captors. But joining this team is no easy task. It requires being accepted into the military, attaining Olympic-level fitness, and then being selected for the training, which has a staggering 90 percent attrition rate. It doesn't matter. His mind is made up—he has to do this. Joining this team, the Navy SEALs, emerges as his objective—a concrete goal that serves the larger purpose of his life.

But how? He begins to research different ways to join the Navy, reads everything he can about the SEALs, and starts a rigorous workout regimen to maximize his chances. Sometimes, it feels like he is veering off course, but the detours are just steps toward positioning himself better to achieve the objective. This clear goal enables him to set meaningful horizons and make progress each day.

That kid was me. My journey wasn't perfect—there were setbacks such as not getting into the Naval Academy, failing the first physical readiness test, and being told my childhood asthma would derail me. But I kept my eyes on the finish line, making every decision—big or small—with the objective in mind. Eventually, a full seven years after setting the initial goal, I crossed the finish line and achieved what had once seemed impossible. I was a Navy SEAL.

And then, of course, the real work began.

PURPOSE MADE CONCRETE

What is your purpose in life? This is a crucial question, one that guides us toward understanding our values, our vision for the world, and our place within it. What ideals inspire you? What vision do you want to bring to life? What legacy do you aspire to leave behind? These reflections help us define our purpose.

However, while having a purpose is powerful, it can sometimes feel too vast and abstract, making it difficult to target.

High performers, those who thrive amid life's uncertainties and challenges, don't just linger on lofty ideals. They transform their purposes into concrete objectives.

As I mentioned in chapter 4, attributes are your fundamental "hows." In chapter 5, we explored identity, your fundamental "whats." Now, let's focus on the third core element: objectives, your fundamental "whys."

Objectives are your purpose made tangible. They are specific goals—granular, actionable, and tied to the current state of affairs in your life. While having a purpose is admirable, to succeed in conditions of uncertainty, challenge, and stress, you must identify and set clear objectives.

OBJECTIVES ARE BEACONS

Life is all about action. We are defined by what we do. Our society often loses sight of this amid endless discussions. We watch the news, share reflections on social media, and debate ethics in comment sections. But in all this talking, we forget the importance of taking action.

Masters of Uncertainty understand this well. They don't

drift with vague purposes; they orient themselves toward specific objectives. They determine what they want to achieve and use that objective as a guiding beacon, especially when faced with decisions—which is all the time. When unpredictability strikes, they keep moving, always guided by their cardinal direction, setting one appropriate horizon after another until they achieve their objective.

Objectives prompt us to ask: What is my Duration, Pathway, and Outcome? You can't DPO your way to a purpose, but you can DPO your way to objectives. Purpose might be making the world safer, but the objective is becoming a Navy SEAL. Purpose might be to survive and thrive, but the objective is to beat cancer. Purpose might be to lose weight and get healthy, but the objective is to run a marathon.

Objectives enable us to break things down into smaller, manageable horizons, which you set moment by moment according to your circumstances. Completing SEAL training can be broken into DPOs like: finish this obstacle course, survive until the next meal, run to that sand berm. Beating cancer becomes: complete this meal, go to the hospital for tests, get a second opinion.

Since objectives often span medium- to long-term time frames, the unpredictable will inevitably strike. You might get sick while attending grad school, break your arm during SEAL training, or face a divorce while raising good kids. What do you do? Hold your objective steady as a cardinal direction.

Set horizons that are still guided by the objective, even if they involve detours. Sometimes reaching the top of a mountain means walking down or around it first. You may lose sight of the peak, feeling like you're moving away from your goal, but maintaining your commitment to the objective is key. Be resolute in your objective but flexible in your approach.

THE UPSHOT: GUIDANCE AND MOTIVATION

Objectives provide both guidance and motivation.

There are 360 degrees you could go in, but you won't get anywhere until you set a cardinal direction and start walking. Objectives are your beacons, offering orientation and clarity for the next steps on your path. "Educate the world" sounds great, but when it comes to daily decisions, "Become a great teacher" is more effective. It's distinct, it's tangible, and offers clear guidance for your choices. This clarity extends to specific horizons you set in pursuit of your objective and influences other life decisions like prioritizing sleep, becoming a morning person, or giving up social media because it hinders your performance.

Objectives are typically stronger motivators than vague purposes because they demand action. You're more likely to get out of bed for a specific, time-sensitive goal than for a broad idea of what matters to you or who you are. Becoming a teacher requires creating a study plan, attending classes, speaking with professors, and revising essays. Waking up with the imperative to act ignites your dopamine circuits. Turning any purpose into an objective gives you a literal biochemical boost, propelling you out the door. As you complete each DPO toward your objective, you experience a dopamine surge that keeps you moving forward.

ACKNOWLEDGE AND RELEASE

The key strategy regarding objectives is simple: acknowledge your objective, then release it. This gives you a cardinal direction to guide you while also freeing you to focus on the present circumstances that must be navigated to reach it.

ACKNOWLEDGE

What is your objective? Maybe you already have one. Acknowledge it. Be clear and specific with yourself about its parameters, any relevant constraints, and your degree of commitment to it.

It's okay to have multiple objectives: professional objectives, personal development objectives, relationship objectives. Simply be clear with yourself on what they are. If you can't specifically articulate an objective, do some soul-searching and clarify it. Make it as concrete as possible. Also, be clear on how you balance your objectives. Be honest with yourself about your priorities. Whenever you're engaged in a task, know which objective you are working toward. Give it your focus. Be present with each objective at the appropriate times. You may wish to parse your time and effort through concrete acts like dividing your workday into specified chunks or color-coding your calendar according to the pursuit of various objectives.

Maybe you don't yet have an objective. Perhaps you have vague intents, things you care about, a vision for the world you wish to bring about. It's time to make this feeling of purpose concrete. If you're unsure about what objectives to set, remember what Masters of Uncertainty do: gather knowledge. What do you know about this already? What do you need to find out? Do you need to research particular career paths? Or maybe you need to accomplish other tasks first, such as paying off loans before making a career jump. Sometimes you aren't 100 percent sure an objective is right for you; the only way to know is to try it. Get the knowledge you need to make a decision, then make it. Select an objective that is concrete and feasible. Begin realizing your purposes.

Remember George from chapter 2, who went from being 450 pounds to an ultrarunner? George felt deeply that he wanted to improve his health. His purpose was to become a healthier, more vibrant person with more energy and ability to participate in life. To make that happen, he needed a concrete objective. He settled on running a marathon. He made this choice through a process of discernment. Once he decided to pursue it, he let it guide his actions.

Know where you're headed. Every time you reach a horizon, zoom out and acknowledge your position relative to your objective. Survey the landscape ahead. You may need to veer east, west, or south for a while. But that's good: east, west, and south are excellent directions to head in as long as they put you in a better position to eventually reach your north.

Many consider the unpredictable a reason to give up. Masters of Uncertainty maintain their objectives and embrace inevitable twists and turns. Set horizons according to what you know and control, and let yourself be guided by the beacon of your cardinal direction.

RELEASE

Once you set an objective, release it. There's no need to dwell. Because it's important to you, you won't forget it. When you zoom out to set horizons, acknowledge it. But the rest of the time, focus on what is happening in the present moment.

You have a long way to go to reach your objective. The unpredictable will strike. You need to be attentive to current circumstances to perform your best.

Say you're participating in an important training program at work, but there's unexpected traffic. You're running late. You may instinctively start obsessing over what's at stake and how important it is to excel at the program. Don't. That's wasted energy and focus. Pause. Stay in the present moment. Assess what you know and control. Be strategic about what actions you can take step-by-step: on the road, while walking through the parking lot, and at the training facility. Optimize the day as best as you can. Allocate your mental resources to performing optimally in the moment you're in. Releasing allows you to recognize and focus on horizons much more clearly.

This also prevents overwhelm, a point I make in chapter 2 when I recommend keeping your eyes off the prize. Dwelling on an objective brings all the effort you'll have to exert to reach it into subconscious awareness, which can dampen dopamine production and create feelings of discouragement. You don't have to focus on beating cancer the whole time. It is often best if you don't. If you are eating the elephant one bite at a time, you don't want to keep staring at the entire elephant. Be in the present moment. Focus on one day at a time. You will optimize the energy you have to keep going and reach the objective.

Releasing fully and giving 100 percent of your attention to the present moment is especially important in acute challenges. Getting through Hell Week required that I release my ultimate goal and give laserlike focus to the present horizon: endure two minutes in the surf, reach the next sand berm, complete the present obstacle course. If I had thought about the entirety of the whole week (let alone the whole six months of SEAL training), I would not have made it through.

Acknowledge, and release.

OBJECTIVES FOR TEAMS

Objectives are particularly crucial for teams; they are the essence of a team. After many years of working with the Navy SEALs and consulting with various high-performing teams, I define a team simply as two or more people working toward a common objective or goal.

My organization is a team working toward empowering individuals and businesses to succeed amid uncertainty. My wife and I are a team working toward raising healthy, responsible, high-character children. My Navy SEAL team was a unit working toward finding terrorists and bringing them to justice.

Objective is everything. In this book, I've dedicated chapters to attributes and identity. Both are crucial for reaching the heights of team performance because they empower teams to reach objectives. Complementary attributes provide teams with the capacities necessary to achieve their objectives. Congruent identities enable teams to share rules and conditions for behavior in pursuit of their objectives.

Set a clear objective for your team. If you have multiple objectives, be extremely clear about which is the focus at any given time. Every member must know this and use it as their cardinal direction. Dynamic subordination is a unique leadership model where the team member best suited to lead in any given moment steps up and takes charge. This individual sets a horizon for the whole team. Others may not understand why this horizon was set, but they follow directives unhesitatingly because they trust that the leader is charting a course guided by the cardinal direction. No matter how far east, west, or south a leader takes a team, all know they are moving into a better position to succeed. Decisions can be unilateral and the follow-through instantaneous because of clear, mutually acknowledged objectives.

I describe more about the dynamic subordination leadership model and how to reach the heights of team performance in chapter 7.

KEY POINTS: CHAPTER 6

1. **Set Clear Objectives:** Having a clear and specific goal is crucial for achieving success, especially in the face of uncertainty and challenges. For example, I was guided by my objective to a Navy SEAL, and George was guided by his objective to run a marathon. Each provided us with direction and motivation.

2. **Transform Purpose into Tangible Objectives:** High performers don't just dwell on lofty ideals; they convert their purposes into concrete, actionable objectives. This transformation makes their goals specific and feasible, helping them navigate uncertainty and stress more effectively.

3. **Objectives as Beacons of Guidance and Motivation:** Objectives act as beacons, providing clarity and orientation for decision-making. They break down larger goals into manageable horizons, ensuring steady progress even when faced with unpredictable circumstances. This approach helps maintain focus and motivation.

4. **Acknowledge and Release Strategy:** The key strategy for managing objectives involves acknowledging your

objective to set a clear direction and then releasing it to focus on present circumstances. This dual approach helps prevent overwhelm and ensures that mental resources are optimally allocated to current tasks, enhancing performance and resilience.

PART III

CREATING MASTERS OF UNCERTAINTY

Every group aspires to be a high-performing team, yet many fall short.

Businesses worldwide exemplify this struggle. They are often teeming with talent, boasting more advanced degrees, skills, and experiences than ever before. Despite this, they often display poor adaptability, low trust, slower pace, missed targets, and underwhelming performance.

A high-performing team excels not only in favorable conditions but also when faced with adversity and unpredictability. The reality is that all teams can achieve high performance. A key reason many teams remain stuck in mediocrity is their failure to account for uncertainty. They rely on outdated leadership models designed for predictable situations, which results in inefficiency, sluggishness, disorganization, and disempowerment. Naturally, performance suffers.

However, when you build your team with the unpredictable nature of business and life in mind, you unlock new levels of performance. You fully harness the potential of each member, creating a synergy where the whole is greater than the sum of its parts.

In this final section, I will guide you through the process of implementing the Mastering Uncertainty Method with your team. Chapter 7 delves into dynamic subordination and how to implement it, including new norms for communication and leadership roles. Chapter 8 focuses on building the deep trust essential for any team's success. Chapter 9 offers strategies for establishing and sustaining a high-performing team culture that thrives over the long term.

While this part of the book emphasizes business teams, the principles apply to all types of teams. A team is simply a group of two or more people working toward a common goal or objective. Whether it's a couple striving for happiness, friends organizing weekly meetups, or volunteers aiming to maximize their impact, all can benefit from these insights.

Regardless of your team's size, nature, identity, or objectives, these are the elements you need to harness your natural abilities and master uncertainty. By the end of these three chapters, your team will have the tools to complement each other's strengths and weaknesses, become greater than the sum of your parts, and consistently achieve top performance—together.

CHAPTER 7

DYNAMIC SUBORDINATION

The Model

As the team of Navy SEALs was approaching the bin Laden compound, one of their helicopters crashed. This was the first of many moments when the well-laid plan had to be discarded, forcing the team to adapt to new circumstances. Throughout the mission (as with most missions), they encountered one curveball after another, any of which could have led to disaster. Yet none did. The team not only achieved their objective but also ensured every member returned home safely.

These men demonstrated the highest possible level of performance. How did they do it? First, each individual was a Master of Uncertainty. But more importantly, they employed a unique leadership model that enables top performers to unite and exceed the sum of their parts: dynamic subordination.

Dynamic subordination is team synergy at its finest. Team members remain present and move in unison, working seamlessly to enhance one another's strengths and buttress weaknesses. When one team member's specific skills or attributes are needed, they step up and lead. The others then automatically move to support them fully. Once their particular expertise is no longer required, they step back, allowing someone else to take the lead. This ensures that the most capable person for the current task or challenge is always at the forefront, taking the fullest possible advantage of each member's strengths.

THE SUBOPTIMALITY OF TRADITIONAL LEADERSHIP MODELS

This type of complementarity and performance is unattainable with the traditional leadership models prevalent in businesses today.

The most common, yet often least effective, traditional leadership model is the hierarchical pyramid, or the "I am your leader; you work for me" approach. This classic structure features a leader at the top with widening layers of subordinates below. It's highly bureaucratic, which significantly limits speed and efficiency. Communication is slow and cumbersome, as it must constantly filter up to the top and back down again. This model operates on minimal trust, designed for an "I say; you do" environment, relying heavily on rank and hierarchy.

In contrast, a high-performing, dynamically subordinating team bases each member's contribution not on rank but on their expertise and proximity to the problem.

Another approach is the flat model, or the "We all work together" style. This model eschews rank and hierarchy and places everyone at the same level, at least in theory. It offers benefits like fostering agency, creativity, and initiative among team members. However, it often lacks clarity of who is actually "in charge," which delays decisions while responsibilities bounce around without a definitive decision-maker. Additionally, actions taken at one end may go unnoticed at the other, leading to inadvertent silos that hinder communication, leadership swapping, and role switching.

Conversely, dynamic subordination ensures fluid communication and transparent information-sharing, allowing rapid adjustments and contributions from all members.

Lastly, there's the upside-down pyramid, or the "I am your leader; I work for you" model. Robert Greenleaf's "servant leadership" philosophy advocates for leaders who inspire, enable, and serve their team members. This approach effectively empowers innovation, creativity, and performance. Of the three traditional models, this is arguably the best—but it's still not ideal for top performance.

In high-performance teams, the burden of leadership is distributed among members and doesn't rest on just one person, allowing for both long-term performance (no one gets burned out) and diversity of thought in decision-making. Dynamic subordination leverages the strengths of each team member in real time, ensuring the most qualified individual leads based on the current needs, thereby optimizing performance and cohesion.

THE LEADERSHIP MODEL FOR UNCERTAINTY

In a world where chaos is the norm and change is constant, dynamic subordination stands out as the most effective leadership model. This approach ensures that the team member best equipped to tackle an unpredictable problem takes charge, while the rest follow and support. As circumstances shift, so does leadership, with the new most suitable person stepping up. This fluid transition keeps the team agile, always putting its best foot forward. The collective expertise and abilities of the team members combine in perfect synergy, making the whole greater than the sum of its parts.

Dynamic subordination is essentially a continuous dance between leading and following, something I also like to call "alpha hopping."

Consider how a commercial airline operates. It's universally accepted that the captain is in command. But what happens when the plane is taxiing and maintenance reports a critical issue? The pilot defers to the expertise of the maintenance crew, trusting their judgment. When the plane returns to the gate and passengers must deplane, the flight attendants take the lead, managing the situation according to established protocols. This illustrates the core principle of dynamic subordination: team members defer to each other's expertise as needed, ensuring the best outcome for the team.

This leadership style is defined by real-time conditions, making it the ideal model for managing uncertainty. As the team morphs into whatever shape is required at any given moment, it optimizes not just its ability to face external conditions but also the crucial (and often overlooked) internal conditions of motivation, energy, and overall health. When individual members take the lead, they feel a sense of accomplishment, boosting their motivation and confidence. When they step back, they have time to recharge. This balance keeps the team functioning at peak performance, ready to face the endless game of navigating uncertainty.

MOVING HORIZONS IN DYNAMICALLY SUBORDINATING TEAMS

Dynamically subordinating teams are made up of Masters of Uncertainty. They navigate uncertainty using the same process of moving horizons (shaping DPOs) that individuals do. They stay grounded in the present, focus on what they know and control, and decide step-by-step on the best next move.

The key difference for teams is in choosing the horizon. This is where dynamic subordination diverges from traditional leadership models. In traditional models, information flows through a chain of command before decisions are made. Typically, as exemplified in the top-down pyramid model, information moves up to a boss and then back down to subordinates. Sometimes in flat or upside-down pyramid organizations, a vote is required before taking action, which is cumbersome and time-consuming.

In dynamically subordinating teams, the person closest to the problem and most capable steps up and crafts the DPO and decides on the next horizon. Everyone else follows. It is simple, fluid, agile, and immediate: adaptable to real conditions in real time.

But how do the right people know to step up, and how do others know to follow?

They rely on three essential kinds of knowledge: that of the objective, that of current circumstances, and that of one another.

KNOWLEDGE OF OBJECTIVE

The power of a shared objective cannot be overstated. Without a clear goal or direction, group efforts are frenetic. A flock of birds flies south for the winter because they share this objective, regardless of which bird leads at any moment. The shared goal provides order and guidance. Teams function the same way: they are driven and guided by a common goal.

KNOWLEDGE OF CURRENT CIRCUMSTANCES

When you're alone, you are the only person viewing and assessing circumstances, so making decisions about horizons is relatively straightforward. You personally assess what's happening, then decide what to do about it.

In a team, understanding current circumstances is more complex. Each team member has a different perspective. They often literally see different events unfold in real time. For dynamic subordination to work, team members must disseminate and be transparent about their understanding. The team member with the most insight, usually the closest to the problem, steps up to set the horizon. Those nearby support this new leader: they receive their information and then communicate the current action to the rest of the team. This ensures everyone understands the situational picture as quickly as possible.

KNOWLEDGE OF ONE ANOTHER

On your own, you decide on the best path and outcome based on your strengths and weaknesses. In a team, decisions rely on a shared understanding of individual roles, expected contributions, strengths, and weaknesses. With this knowledge, team members instantly recognize who should step up during uncertainty. High-performing teams establish clear expectations for leadership in different situations, discuss contingency plans, and telegraph their strengths and weaknesses. When unexpected events arise, the most suitable person leads based on their abilities, and others follow and support.

High-performing teams expect events to deviate from plans. In true complexity, the teams with the most intimate knowledge of each other's abilities shine. They dynamically subordinate with great fluidity, capable of operating even outside their emergency plans, always ready to put their best foot forward.

This process of moving horizons can happen very rapidly when called for, as long as there is transparency of information, efficient communication, clarity of roles and abilities, and trust in each other.

WHERE TO START

Implementing dynamic subordination might seem daunting at first, but there are four key areas to focus on to get started.

1. BUILD TRUST

Trust is the bedrock of dynamic subordination. Team members must trust each other to step up and step back appropriately and to fulfill their assigned tasks. This level of trust is vital and is the focus of chapter 8. Without trust, the fluid leadership and support that dynamic subordination requires cannot function.

2. ESTABLISH COMMUNICATION

Immediate, full, and transparent access to information for all team members is crucial. Communication norms should be clear, rapid, and effective, without obstacles created by hierarchies or silos.

Ensure that information is instantly available to everyone on the team. When information needs to be shared, establish norms for communicating quickly and effectively. Transparency is essential; any barriers to the situational picture can prevent team members from stepping up when needed or from knowing when others have done so. This can lead to redundancies, waste, conflict, and mistakes. Real-time access to information empowers team members to know what's happening, understand others' actions, and respond appropriately.

3. BE VULNERABLE

Beyond recognizing abilities and attributes, mutual, nonjudgmental acknowledgment is vital. The team must be accustomed to sharing strengths and weaknesses openly, understanding that vulnerability means being transparent about both. Leaders should share their personal strengths and weaknesses and encourage others to do the same, fostering a culture where this is actively practiced.

As an example, consider the benefits my wife and I gain from knowing each other's attributes. She knows I am patient and deliberate, though sometimes slow to act. I know she is naturally impatient (which isn't a bad thing). In parenting, there are moments that demand patience, such as teaching teens how to drive. In these situations, I take the lead. However, when a child shows symptoms of illness, my wife's impatience becomes an asset, enabling us to take swift and necessary action.

The best way to be transparent about one's qualities, especially under pressure, is to know what they are. Have each team member complete an attribute assessment and share the results. Openly discuss strengths and weaknesses and which situations may require specific attributes. This is crucial for when uncertainty is high and the team must operate outside typical expectations. Unpredictability is always a factor, and mutual awareness of strengths and weaknesses helps the team put its best foot forward.

4. CREATE LOW-RISK OPPORTUNITIES FOR PRACTICE

Allow team members to practice stepping up when the risk is low. They might perform well and gain confidence. If they don't, they can learn and improve for next time.

This step is how dynamic subordination takes root. As a commander, I once encouraged a troop member to lead his first parachute boat drop during an exercise in Virginia Beach. As I observed him going through the process, I began to suspect he would miss the target, but after determining the risk of incident and injury was low, I let him proceed. He made the mistake, but we debriefed as a team, discussing what went well and what didn't. We showed him we supported his learning process. This paid off in the long run. The next time he needed to take the lead on a boat drop, we were on a real mission on the other side of the world—and he nailed it.

THE PERSON "IN CHARGE"

Dynamic subordination doesn't eliminate the need for someone to be in charge. Call this person what you will: commanding officer, CEO, boss. This individual has three critical roles:

1. CULTIVATE TRUST

Those in charge must behave in ways that inspire trust in others and reward such behavior within the team. Trust is foundational for dynamic subordination, allowing team members to confidently step up and step back as needed. This means that the leader must model this behavior first, then also reward it when it happens. A leader that never steps back allowing others to shine isn't a leader—they are a dictator.

2. DELEGATE RESPONSIBILITY

Those in charge should provide opportunities for their team to succeed and, importantly, to fail and learn. This process builds a team of dynamically subordinating individuals who periodically feel confident stepping up. Allowing team members to take the lead in various situations fosters their growth and prepares them for future challenges. It builds future leaders.

3. MAINTAIN ACCOUNTABILITY

Regardless of the measure of success achieved in any horizon or task, the person in charge must own the result and demonstrate support for the team. They should stand by their team members, ensuring they feel supported and valued. While responsibility can be delegated, accountability cannot. Those who delegate responsibility without owning the accountability aren't true *leaders*; they're merely in charge.

REAL LEADERSHIP

Finally, these three roles are best implemented when the person in charge strives to become a real leader.

Real leadership contrasts sharply with a traditional mentality common among those in charge that I call *driving*. *Drivers* see themselves as in control of everything and treat their organizations like systems or machines. When things don't go as planned, they typically respond by punishing or replacing team members. They use rewards sparingly to motivate performance. They operate tight ships and often micromanage, forcing team members to carry out their vision unilaterally.

Drivers treat team members as replaceable parts. An immutable truth, however, is that if you treat people as if they don't matter, they will act accordingly. They will deliver only the minimum required, and no more. When punishment fails to correct or motivate, drivers often respond by punishing more. This further disempowers and demotivates team members, stifling initiative, creativity, and overall performance.

In contrast, team members naturally want to go the extra mile when they are invited to and inspired from the bottom up rather than manipulated from the top down. True leaders recognize this and see themselves as part of a larger whole, like an organ in a living, breathing body. They understand that all parts of a team must be nourished to thrive. While those in charge have the broadest vantage point and are accountable for the whole team, true leaders acknowledge that others possess skills and insights they may miss. They rely fully on their team's expertise.

True leaders don't celebrate or elevate themselves. Instead, they set the example for how they want their team members to perform. They seek opportunities to help and serve, considering no task beneath them. They go the extra mile to serve the mission shared by everyone. True leaders don't seek to stand out or to be recognized as the leader. In fact, they don't even give themselves the label "leader." It is given to them by their team members. True leaders are identifiable by having inspired followers eager to identify with them and be on their team.

THE REASONS FOR DYNAMIC SUBORDINATION

Dynamic subordination is counterintuitive for many in our culture. It's against the grain. It bucks traditional norms about leadership, hierarchies, and chains of command. But those who employ it don't do so for the sake of being different. It's done for the superior performance, plain and simple. It's for how much more consistently they hit or exceed old benchmarks. It's for the new heights of fluidity, agility, and securing desired outcomes. Most importantly—it's done for those moments of challenge and uncertainty, when maximum perspective and participation are required.

Round out the set of competencies you need to implement dynamic subordination by learning about team trust in chapter 8 and learning how to build and maintain high-performing team culture in chapter 9.

KEY POINTS: CHAPTER 7

1. **Dynamic Subordination Leadership Model:** Dynamic subordination is a leadership model where the team member with the most relevant attributes and skills, as well as proximity to the problem, steps up to lead while others support. This model ensures the team adapts

fluidly to real-time conditions, optimizing performance and leveraging each member's strengths.

2. **Limitations of Traditional Leadership Models:** Traditional leadership models, such as the hierarchical pyramid, the flat model, and the upside-down pyramid, have significant limitations in dynamic and unpredictable environments. These models often suffer from slow communication, lack of clear leadership, and burnout of a single leader. In contrast, dynamic subordination distributes leadership responsibilities, enhancing agility and effectiveness.

3. **Essential Knowledge for Dynamic Subordination:** To work, teams need shared knowledge in three areas: the objective, current circumstances, and each other's strengths and weaknesses. This shared understanding allows the right person to step up and lead in response to current challenges, ensuring that the team remains cohesive and effective.

4. **Implementing Dynamic Subordination:** Successful implementation requires building trust, establishing clear communication, fostering vulnerability, and creating low-risk opportunities for practice. Leaders should cultivate trust, delegate responsibility, and

maintain accountability to support a high-performing team capable of navigating uncertainty and achieving its objectives.

CHAPTER 8

TRUST

The Frame

It was the spring of 1997 on San Clemente Island, a secluded US military training ground off the coast of San Diego. I was deep into the third phase of BUD/S (Basic Underwater Demolition / SEAL) training, the initial crucible for aspiring Navy SEALs. Known to us simply as "the island," this remote locale was where we endured our final five weeks of intense preparation.

Seventy miles from the Californian mainland, San Clemente Island allowed us to conduct live-fire exercises, land and underwater demolitions, and a slew of grueling activities without disturbing the unsuspecting public. The island also had a nickname among students: "the place where no one can hear you scream." Daily meals weren't a given; they were earned through arduous physical feats including a seventy-foot rope climb, a brutal mix of twenty-five pull-ups, fifty push-ups, and twenty-five dips, or the dreaded hill run.

The hill run was the pinnacle of our torment. It was a sprint up a steep, unforgiving hill to touch a monument at the summit and then a precipitous dash back down, racing against a clock with ever-decreasing time limits each week. For added punishment, instructors had devised "flights," where we lugged a seventy-five-pound metal pallet on our backs, along with our gear, up and down the hill. It was a sinister twist on the classic run, reserved specifically for mistakes, breaking rules, or simply the amusement of the instructors.

One spring afternoon, just as we were on the brink of graduation and preparing to leave for San Diego, the voice of one of our instructors shattered our euphoria: "Class 210, muster on the flight line!" Instructor Goodman, ironically not a "good man" that day, had an impossible (and insane) order for us: break the fastest hill run record, but do it as "flights," with the heavy pallets on our back and in full gear. The mood shifted to frustration, especially once he announced we'd keep running flights until the record was broken.

My temper flared, and although I didn't say anything, my nonverbal cues obviously caught Goodman's eye. When Goodman singled me out, asking if I had a problem with his orders, I blurted out with frustration, "Yes, I do. This is stupid, and someone's going to get hurt." Goodman, with a sadistic smirk, pressed further. "Why do you care?" I stood my ground.

"Because they're my guys, and I don't want them to get hurt."

Silence fell, thick as a morgue, and suddenly I felt the weight of my words. After an eternity, Goodman relented, surprisingly offering, "Okay. Since Ensign Diviney has a problem, we'll run back to the barracks and watch movies instead." The relief was palpable. We scrambled back, eager to seize the unexpected reprieve.

While the moment felt exceptionally good, I don't even remember what movies we ended up watching—but that's not the point of this story. The point came seventeen years later, when I bumped into two guys from my BUD/S class I hadn't seen since graduation. We were reminiscing when one of them said, "Hey, sir, remember when you stood up to Goodman on the flight line?" I hadn't thought about it in years but recalled it instantly.

"That was awesome," they both said. "We'd follow you anywhere and trust you anytime."

THE FOUR DOMAINS OF TRUST

Most leaders understand that trust is key to performance. But saying it's crucial is an understatement—it's the bedrock of any team. Without it, you can't even get off the ground, let alone dynamically subordinate. You also can't function in uncertainty, which is essential in the modern business landscape.

Thankfully, trust isn't that complex: it's a belief you form through observing evidence of trustworthiness. Many people mistake trust for a feeling. We often hear or say, "I feel like I trust them" or "It feels like I can trust this." But a feeling is just an emotion, which can be fleeting, mercurial. Trust goes beyond that. It's a belief. A conviction. A feeling rationalized or justified to the extent that you can act on it.

I consider beliefs to be emotions that have been rationalized or justified. It doesn't matter if a belief is correct or how it's become justified—only that it has. Once it has, it's become a belief. Trust is the decision to "believe in" someone or something.

Thanks to free will, belief can't be forced. No one can make anyone else believe anything. So we can't "make" anyone trust us. All we can do is create an environment that exhibits the behaviors of trust and gives them the opportunity to decide to trust us.

Building trust is about creating such an environment, which you do with your behavior. Behavior is key. People don't decide to trust based on what you say, but what you do. If I had stayed quiet when provoked by Goodman but told my fellow trainees later that I'd been concerned for them, they would likely have appreciated the sentiment. But I took action that put my own well-being on the line—and that was compelling evidence I could be trusted.

When I worked with friends at the Chapman & Co. Leadership Institute and we researched trust, we found there are four components, or domains, of building and sustaining trust: competence, consistency, character, and compassion.

Competence: Do the "thing" right. This is straightforward—it's about being able to do something correctly or as expected. Whether it's driving, leading a sales meeting, throwing a ball, parenting, or being in a relationship, you need to show you can do what you're supposed to. Doing tasks in line with others' expectations is crucial for trust. Society often helps us trust each other's competency through accreditations. For example, we trust other drivers (most of the time) because we can reasonably assume they've gone through the process of obtaining a license. On a team, you must demonstrate your competence and provide opportunities for teammates to demonstrate theirs.

Consistency: Do the "thing" right over time. Again, simple and straightforward. Showing competence repeatedly builds trust. Society helps here too. Rules and laws ensure consistent behavior—we trust drivers to stop at red lights and go at green ones. On a team, rules can help, but you must show that they are consistently followed. Sometimes there is competence without consistency, and that isn't enough. If your brakes work only three out of five times, you won't trust them.

Character: Do the right thing. Character essentially means loyalty to the right thing, whatever that means for your context. Several attributes play a role in character, but integrity is the most important. Integrity means being whole, congruent, and consistent with a set of values. It's the belief that "I know you will do the right thing." Integrity varies across cultures and contexts because the right thing can be subjective. "Doing the right thing" in a Boy Scout troop differs from "doing the right thing" among inmates. On your team, "doing the right thing" has its own meaning. Remaining loyal to that is key to building and sustaining deeper trust.

Compassion: Do the right thing because you care. This means acting in ways that show you care about team members as people. Compassionate relationships are our deepest relationships—family, friends, tribes, and select teams. In these relationships, we believe others will go the extra mile, do whatever it takes, and sometimes even put themselves at risk for us. Compassion that's backed up with compassionate action forges trust at these most significant levels.

A trusting relationship can start with any of the four domains, but only when you have all four does the deepest, most durable, long-lasting trust exist. Consider this example:

It's late, and you're ready to head home after a fun night out with friends. You call a cab, and it shows up within minutes. You jump in, exchange quick pleasantries with the driver, and the car pulls into the street. After driving about a hundred yards, the driver runs into a telephone pole. A couple of days later, you find yourself in the exact same situation: you call a cab, and it's the same driver from the other night. Would you get back into that car? Probably not. You wouldn't trust that driver.

Now rewind the scenario. Imagine the driver is your father, mother, sibling, or spouse. Would you get back in the car after the first accident? You likely would. Why? Because with the first driver, you only had two elements of trust: the consistency of the cab company and the presumed competence of the driver (since he obviously has a license). When the driver's competence faltered, your trust vanished. With your family member behind the wheel instead, you start out with all four elements. When their competence has taken a hit, the other three elements might sustain your trust enough for you to get in the car.

Reflecting on what happened over twenty years ago on the island, I see now that I was inadvertently building trust. I was one of eight officers out of thirty-eight graduates (from a starting class of 170). Through the course of training, I had shown the competence and consistency required of a Navy SEAL trainee.

That was helpful and important. But stepping out of line (however unconsciously) displayed both character and compassion. The combination of all four elements cemented a trust powerful enough to last over seventeen years of absence.

Creating an environment with all four elements fosters a very resilient trust.

DYNAMIC SUBORDINATION AND VULNERABILITY

There is one final trust-building action leaders of dynamically subordinating teams must take: be vulnerable first. Because showing weakness is often stigmatized, vulnerability on high-performing teams means showing strengths and weaknesses—wearing it all on your sleeve. Dynamic subordination *requires* this type of vulnerability. Team members must understand one another's strengths and weaknesses to identify the right moments to step up and step back and therefore always put their best foot forward. The more members understand about one another, the more swiftly and effectively this happens.

As the leader, you must foster an environment where vulnerable sharing happens and is acted upon—and you must go first. You must model—and reward—the behavior you want to see more of. There is no alternative. No other strategies will work if this one isn't in place. Be fully transparent and vulnerable about yourself. Share and display not just your strengths but also your weaknesses. Don't pretend to have attributes or abilities you don't possess. Ask for help when you're not the best fit for something.

When someone else is better equipped to handle a situation, openly say to them, in front of the whole team, "I need you." These three words are the most important any leader can say.

Doing this shows the rest of the team that it's not just okay but also good to acknowledge your own limitations and step back when you're not best suited to a task. It's also crucial to reward others when they do the same, as it reinforces the value of vulnerability within your team. Over time, team members will increasingly feel more safe and confident stepping up and back according to their strengths and weaknesses, making dynamic subordination possible.

TRUST AND PERFORMANCE

Dynamic subordination is the leadership model best suited to the uncertain conditions of life and business. It enables teams to take swift and effective action, no matter what comes their way—and it does not happen without trust.

Remember: trust cannot be forced, only invited through action and behavior. Provide team members with evidence they can trust, and they will trust. Go first. Be consistent. Demonstrate and establish competency, consistency, character, and compassion. Make sure these aren't just values you voice but actions you take. People trust when given reason to.

Facilitate trust, and you're nearly 100 percent of the way to a high-performing team. I explain the remaining components of establishing and maintaining a high-performing team culture in the next and final chapter.

KEY POINTS: CHAPTER 8

1. **The Four Domains of Trust:** Trust is built on four key components: competence (doing the task correctly), consistency (repeatedly demonstrating competence), character (doing the right thing), and compassion (showing you care). These elements together create the deepest and most durable trust.

2. **Importance of Trust in Teams:** Trust is the foundational element of any high-performing team, especially necessary for dynamic subordination. Without trust, teams cannot function effectively in uncertain environments, which is critical in both military and business settings.

3. **Trust through Vulnerability:** Leaders must be the first to show vulnerability, openly sharing their strengths and weaknesses. This behavior sets a precedent for team members to do the same, fostering an environment where individuals feel safe to step up or step back based on their abilities, thus facilitating dynamic subordination.

4. **Building Trust through Action:** Trust is built not through words but through consistent behavior. Leaders must demonstrate competence, consistency, character, and compassion in their actions. By doing so, they create an environment where trust can flourish, enabling the team to perform at its best under uncertain conditions.

CHAPTER 9

CULTURE

The Engine

I've described dynamic subordination and the trust necessary to sustain it, but there are three other key elements of building and maintaining team culture necessary for long-term thriving:

1. Establish and leverage team identity.
2. Properly evaluate team performance.
3. Bring in the right team members.

TEAM IDENTITY: SERVING VALUES THROUGH ACTION

As explained in chapter 5 on identities, the words "I am" are the two most powerful in the English language. We each have fundamental "I am" statements, both conscious and subconscious, and they shape our behavior, especially when we face challenges. This concept applies to teams as well. To be able to reach objectives in uncertain conditions, it is crucial to understand, clarify, and establish a shared identity.

Team identities can be thought of as "values plus action." What does your team value, and what behavior is appropriate for serving those values? Ideally, a team or organization's values outline what it means to be part of that group, establishing the rules and conditions for that identity. Take the Girl Scouts, for example. Every young lady who joins makes a promise to live by the "Girl Scout Law," which includes the following values:

- Be honest and fair, friendly and helpful, considerate and caring, courageous and strong, and responsible for what you say and do.
- Respect yourself and others, authority, and resources.
- Make the world a better place and be a sister to every Girl Scout.

By making this pledge, a young lady adopts the shared identity of a Girl Scout, guiding her and the group in every environment.

If everyone on a team commits to an identity they truly care about, they are instantly bound together, sharing not just values but also specific rules and conditions by which they uphold those values. This is why many organizations display their values prominently. Rallying around shared values and working together to uphold them is motivating and improves trust, morale, and performance. However, many organizations make the mistake of being too vague with their values. They fail to define them properly and to supply specific enough rules and conditions for upholding them, thus missing out on the full power of identity.

CONSCIOUS VERSUS SUBCONSCIOUS IDENTITY

The rules and conditions around being on a team or in a group can form either consciously or subconsciously. For instance, friend groups often develop unwritten rules and conditions for behavior, such as how often they call each other, without ever explicitly discussing them. Similarly, a team of marines or a football team might have unspoken rules about how they communicate. A group of inmates might have strict codes against snitching. All of these play a role in the shared identity and what it means for the members to be a part of this group.

Both consciously and subconsciously formed rules can be powerful—but only consciously created rules can be controlled. Teams must be deliberate, intentional, and explicit about the rules and conditions established for identity. Otherwise, a couple of things might happen:

1. Bad rules and conditions might be created.
2. Even good rules and conditions might not be known by everyone.

While "unspoken" rules are often part of every team, to consistently thrive in uncertainty and dynamically subordinate, you, along with your team or the leaders of any organization or group you're a part of, must intentionally craft the team identity. The strongest team identities are those that are intentionally chosen and then embraced by all members.

THE SPECIFICITY FACTOR

While values are essential for building a shared identity, it's crucial to consider how we establish them. Many teams or organizations create a few key words or short statements, display them prominently, and call them "our core values." This approach rarely works because it often remains too vague and subjective when it comes to actual behavior.

Consider a team that states one of their values as "Excellence." How does one "behave" with excellence? Each person's interpretation of excellence can vary significantly. Without clear rules and conditions defining how to embody the value of "excellence," team members might perform a wide range of actions, leading to conflict among them and confusion among external stakeholders about who you are and what you stand for.

Specific actions create clarity, which fosters proper and predictable behavior. Just as all team members need to understand their respective roles and contributions to appropriately step up and back while pursuing objectives, they also need clear expectations for behavior in all circumstances, especially during uncertainty. This clarity gives them confidence in their decisions and trust in others to act as expected, even or especially when operating outside normal conditions. When everyone knows what kind of behavior they can expect from one another, there is increased speed, trust, agility, and performance.

A common concern among business leaders is whether the concept of identity applies to their teams. They might argue that their business team is too mundane to have a powerful identity. They might say, "We're not the Navy SEALs; we're a company where people work from nine to five to pay the bills. We sell products or services that don't seem particularly emotionally rich." However, this is a misconception.

Any organization can have powerful and motivating values

and identities. Values are often about not what you do but how you do it. You can build values like empathy, vulnerability, and honesty into your identity. Your purpose can be transforming or serving the world simply by doing your best, exhibiting character, and doing honorable work. Identity doesn't have to be about what service you provide; it can be about how you provide it.

Be as specific as possible with the rules and conditions according to which your team acts, with statements like:

- Ensure the client has what they need, even if it's not our product.

- Always make your best effort to be on time and apologize if late.

- Replace printer paper when low.

These behaviors, which exemplify values of care and conscientiousness, don't need to be Herculean—they just need to be stated. The benefits of such specificity include consistency, higher morale, easier communication, increased trust, and rapid and effective dynamic subordination.

Finally, specific actions are crucial for *all* teams: not just professional or organized ones but also interpersonal relationships. Consider a marriage. You and your spouse might value time together, but what are your rules and conditions for spending that time together? Do you put away your cell phones or carve out specific time blocks? You might also value clear communication, but what does that mean for how you talk to or text each other? The more specific you can be about actions that support your relationship and shared values, the better you can set proper expectations and trust each other in certain and uncertain conditions alike.

BEYOND VALUES TO "I AM" STATEMENTS

Once you've established the values and the corresponding rules and conditions for your team identity, solidify that identity by creating a series of "I am" statements. Masters of Uncertainty understand how powerful the words "I am" are for motivation and purpose, so they deliberately frame the team's values, rules, and conditions around this idea. Leaders of the highest-performing teams craft specific "I am" statements that every team member can genuinely embrace as their own.

When I was the commanding officer of a Navy SEAL squadron, I needed a way to firmly establish and remind the command of its identity. Before taking charge, I created a list of "I am" statements for the team and reviewed them with the officer and enlisted leadership to ensure their agreement. Each "I am" reflected a value that described or implied an action.

Upon taking command, I presented the list as our command philosophy—essentially our values. This approach ensured that instead of having nebulous and vague values or a philosophy that felt like a lecture, each team member could read these statements and immediately embody the squadron identity. This shaped behavior at all levels.

Here are a few of the "I am" statements we created (there were ten in total):

- I am a surgical warrior: the top 1 percent in my field.
- I am disciplined in all aspects of my life—discipline drives me to superior performance.
- I am self-aware. Relentless in my self-discovery, I openly hold myself accountable for my strengths and weaknesses.
- I am audacious. My greatest fear is letting down those who trust in me.
- I am creative, agile, and adaptive. Complacency is my most formidable enemy.
- I am humble—for humility elicits admiration and trust in those I protect and abject terror in my enemy.

The final statement forged the command's identity to the individual:

- I am SEAL Team ## (actual command left out for security purposes).

The idea is to create your own list. Try to use between three and twelve items, but no more, as more than that becomes cumbersome. Focus on what's most important. Conclude your list with an assertion of the identity: "I am [insert team name here]." This is a crucial step because it unifies the behaviors and forges a bond between the individual and the team.

Doing this enables team members to come together in a shared identity and purpose. They are reminded of the clear expectations, rules, and conditions of the team in a powerfully visceral way. They serve their values, living and working together in service of those values. Provide the rules and conditions of behavior to all team members through their shared "I am."

EVALUATING PERFORMANCE

The behaviors on the list of "I am" statements also double as performance evaluation tools. They allow you to clearly see if someone is acting in line with the team's values. Team members must uphold the values with the actions outlined in support of them. If team members operate according to different rules and conditions, they are out of alignment with the identity. Conduct honest and supportive conversations about whether they can start enacting proper behaviors and what it might take to achieve that.

Another key evaluation tool is attribute assessment. When employees underperform, it might be due to poor attribute matching. Is each employee in a role suited to their attribute profile? At one point in my career, I was in charge of a supply team. Half of the team worked on future projects, and the other half worked on administrative tasks. One member of the future projects team was underperforming. After sitting down with her, I quickly realized that her unique attribute profile was much better suited to the administrative team. For example, her high-discernment compartmentalization allowed her to focus on details for long periods of time when conducting excruciating inventories. All I did was shift her over to the admin team, and her performance skyrocketed.

Attribute assessment can also lead to increased satisfaction and engagement, and therefore reduced attrition (whether voluntary or forced), as it's enjoyable to perform tasks at which one naturally excels, and it's challenging, sometimes frustrating or discouraging, to perform tasks for which one is poorly suited.

In some cases, it's possible to develop someone's lagging attributes, though it can take significant effort and time, depending on the situation. Consider coaching and supporting team members in developing certain attributes if it seems likely to be effective.

BRINGING IN THE RIGHT TEAM MEMBERS

One of the biggest mistakes I see managers and headhunters make is hiring solely based on candidates' skills and experiences. Most prioritize what's listed on a résumé. While this information is relevant, it's not the most crucial. What truly matters is the raw self: the candidate's identity and attributes. Identity: Will prospective team members instinctively behave in harmony with the team's needs? Attributes: Do their attributes complement existing team members' and align with those necessary for this team?

Skills can be taught, and experiences can be gained, but attributes and identity are much harder to change and far more important. Focus your hiring on attributes and identity, and your team will be more sustainably able to perform as needed, especially when it counts.

In any instance when you may need a new team member, pause first. Assess present conditions and what is possible with your existing team. Conduct attribute assessment and matching; use what's revealed to reshuffle team members to optimize their fit for their roles. This process has a double benefit: it optimizes the performance of present team members, and it provides a clear picture of any gaps that need to be filled. This is when you should hire, and these are the gaps you should hire for.

While seeking candidates with attribute fit, ensure that their personal identity is congruent with the team identity. Every member of a team has a distinct identity off the team. That's not a bad thing. What is necessary is that there is no significant conflict between an individual's core personal identity (or identities) and the identity of the team. All members must be able and eager to opt into the shared identity without any other identities creating inner tension or conflict. That way, when uncertainty strikes and all default to acting out more instinctive sets of rules and conditions, the team identity remains natural to uphold and the attendant rules and conditions natural to follow.

BUILDING AND MAINTAINING A SOLID FOUNDATION

The big mistake in building team culture is not going deep enough. It's painting core values on the wall absent deeper implications or facilitating bonding with fun activities and team-building exercises without digging into the reasons behind them. While at the surface level, these activities can help with familiarity, there needs to be an effort to reach down to the deeper, foundational levels of shared identity and complementarity attributes that are necessary for teams to dynamically subordinate.

Establish your team's identity and empower team members to perform optimally in appropriate and complementary roles. For a high-performing team culture that thrives in uncertain conditions, you must prioritize establishing this deeper, more solid, and more powerful foundation. Discern values and decide on corresponding behaviors. Write a meaningful and clear set of "I ams." Empower team members with roles that suit them. Keep it all going with hiring and evaluation processes based on identity and attributes. You will foster a team culture that enables dynamic subordination and raises its heights of performance indefinitely.

KEY POINTS: CHAPTER 9

1. **Establish and Leverage Team Identity:** Team identity is crucial for guiding behavior and achieving objectives. It is built on shared values and specific actions that uphold those values. Teams must consciously create and embrace their identity with clear rules and conditions to ensure all members act consistently and predictably, especially under uncertain conditions. Specific "I am" statements can solidify this identity and align individual behaviors with the team's values.

2. **Evaluate Team Performance:** Performance evaluation should be based on how well team members embody the team's values through their actions. Regularly assess whether individuals are aligned with the team's identity and if they are performing tasks suited to their attributes. Address any misalignments through honest conversations and attribute assessments, which can help reassign roles for better performance and satisfaction.

3. **Hire for Attributes and Identity:** When hiring, focus on candidates' attributes and whether their personal identities align with the team's identity. Skills and experiences can be taught, but core attributes and identity are harder to change. Ensure that new hires will naturally fit and enhance the team's dynamic, especially under stress and uncertainty. Conduct attribute assessments to understand existing team capabilities and identify gaps that new hires should fill.

4. **Maintain a Solid Foundation:** Building a high-performing team culture requires going beyond surface-level activities. Deeply establish and maintain a strong foundation of shared values, clear "I am" statements, and complementary roles. This foundation supports dynamic subordination and enables the team

to thrive in uncertain conditions. Regularly revisit and reinforce these elements through hiring, evaluation, and ongoing team development practices.

CONCLUSION

Life is an unpredictable voyage, filled with challenges that test our resilience, adaptability, and courage. These moments of uncertainty are not obstacles to be feared but opportunities to be seized. They are the crucibles in which our true capabilities are forged and refined. By recognizing and cultivating our innate attributes, we equip ourselves to navigate these turbulent waters with confidence and grace.

The journey of self-discovery and growth is ongoing. It requires a commitment to continuous reflection and development. It demands that we remain open to new experiences, willing to learn from our successes and our failures, and ready to adapt to ever-changing circumstances. In this journey, every step, no matter how small, contributes to our overall growth and prepares us for the challenges ahead.

As you move forward, remember that the strength to thrive in uncertainty comes from within. It is rooted in the unique combination of qualities that make you who you are. Trust in your abilities, embrace your journey with all its uncertainties, and strive to perform optimally in every moment. Your journey is yours to shape, and the possibilities are boundless.

Let this be a call to action: to live with purpose, to lead with integrity, and to face the unknown with unwavering determination. The road ahead is open, filled with opportunities waiting to be discovered. Embrace it with enthusiasm, and let your innate potential guide you to new heights of achievement and fulfillment.

In the end, mastering uncertainty is about more than just surviving; it is about thriving. It is about becoming the best version of yourself and helping others to do the same. So go forth, embrace the journey, use this method, and make your mark. Your story is just beginning, and the best is yet to come.

ACKNOWLEDGMENTS

WHENEVER I HEAR anyone speak about writing a book in a casual way, it causes me to chuckle. It is anything but a casual process. It takes time, effort, and loads of support from others. This book was no different.

Stefani Ruper: Thank you for all of your guidance, ideas, conversation, and brilliant writing during this project. It is for certain that this would not have come to fruition without you—I am thrilled that we got to work on it together.

Andrew Huberman: As usual, brother, it's our many conversations and your wonderfully unique and eloquently explained knowledge of neuroscience that inspire me to think in these ways. I highly value our friendship and will always be grateful for it.

My Navy SEAL brothers: To have served among people for whom I always strived to be my best was the highlight of my twenty-one years in the Teams. Although times were both good and bad, it all caused me to show up as the best version of myself, think more deeply, and always master uncertainty.

The Attributes team: None of us are an island—in any endeavor. To have such outstanding teammates now in my new, post-military life is something that continues to drive and inspire me every single day.

Veerle Jenny Monkerhey: For Kristen and me, you are much more than a COO. Your talents and qualities are invaluable in shaping and expanding this company, which began as a mere idea. You bring competence, patience, and balance to our team. We deeply cherish you and hold our friendship in the highest regard. Thank you.

Josh and Connor: Josh—your strength, intelligence, steadiness, and positive demeanor are not only qualities that I admire but also lean on, and you always bring happiness. Connor—your curiosity, open-mindedness, and intelligence continue to astound, impress, and delight me. You are outstanding men, and I am immensely proud to be your father.

Kristen: I've said it before and will continue to for all of my days: you are my lighthouse. But you are also my soulmate, my partner, my princess, and my best friend. There is no one I'd rather be with, and I treasure every moment together. Mastering uncertainty is easy with you—as is every other part of my life. I love you.

ABOUT THE AUTHOR

Rich Diviney is a retired Navy SEAL commander. In a career spanning more than twenty years, he completed more than thirteen overseas deployments—eleven of which were to Iraq and Afghanistan—and served as the officer in charge of selection, assessment, and training for a specialized SEAL command. He also spearheaded the creation of the "Mind Gym" that the SEALs use to train their brains to perform faster, longer, and better, especially in high-stress environments.

Since 2017, he has taught classes and delivered keynote speeches about leadership, optimal performance, and high-performing teams to thousands of business, athletic, and military leaders and to organizations such as Google, McKinsey, American Airlines, the San Francisco 49ers, McLaren Automotive, Adobe, Ernst & Young, Zoom, Bank of America, Lexus, and Deloitte.

Diviney is also the author of the bestselling book *The Attributes: 25 Hidden Drivers of Optimal Performance.*